THE PEOPLE'S STRUGGLE
CAMBODIA REBORN

All the photographs in this book are from the author's private collection

First English-language edition published by the National Assembly of the Kingdom of Cambodia in 2018. First published in the Khmer language by the National Assembly of the Kingdom of Cambodia as *Samdech Akka Moha Ponhea Chakrei Heng Samrin* in 2013. Second edition, *Kamnorthaet Samdech Akka Moha Ponhea Chakrei Heng Samrin Katorsu Rumdos Procheachun neungka Aphiwat Cheath*, with contributions from Say Chhum, Ney Pena, Sim Ka, Cheam Yeap, Vong Sauth, Yi Yon and Keo Piseth, published in 2016.

English translation by San Sarana, Pen Prakath, Heang Thul, Soth Kimsan, Say Amnann and Chan Savel

Editor (Cambodia): Peter Starr
Editor (Singapore): Timothy Auger

First published in 2018
by Editions Didier Millet Pte Ltd
78 Jalan Hitam Manis
Singapore 278488

www.edmbooks.com.sg

Printed in Malaysia by TWP Sdn Bhd

ISBN: 978-981-4610-49-0

THE PEOPLE'S STRUGGLE

CAMBODIA REBORN

HENG SAMRIN

edm EDITIONS DIDIER MILLET

This book is dedicated to the souls of all Cambodians who courageously devoted their lives to national liberation and protecting the motherland.
May they all rest in peace.

Samdech Akka Moha Ponhea Chakrei Heng Samrin

FOREWORD

On the afternoon of 10 May 2012, Samdech Akka Moha Ponhea Chakrei Heng Samrin handed me a draft account of his life experiences, with a view to having it published as a book. Since childhood, Samdech has been of great service to the nation, and has earned enormous respect. The story of his achievements is of great historical value. I therefore recommend this book to anyone interested in the recent history of Cambodia, including not only researchers but also all future generations of Cambodians.

His Excellency Ney Pena
First Vice President,
Senate of the Kingdom of Cambodia
Phnom Penh, May 2018

CONTENTS

ACKNOWLEDGMENTS

This book has been compiled and published with contributions, editing, clarifications and proofreading by Samdech Say Chhum and Their Excellencies Ney Pena, Sim Ka, Dr Cheam Yeap, Vong Sauth, Yi Yon and Keo Piseth.

I would like to wish Their Excellencies the four Buddhist blessings of Longevity (*Ayuk*), Wealth (*Vannak*), Harmony (*Sokhak*) and Strength (*Poleak*).

Samdech Akka Moha Ponhea Chakrei Heng Samrin
President,
National Assembly of the Kingdom of Cambodia
Phnom Penh

EDITORS' ACKNOWLEDGEMENTS

The editors of the English edition would like to acknowledge the valuable assistance provided by Margaret Bywater, His Excellency Chum Sounry, Darryl Collins, Greg Dodds, Helen Jarvis, Michele McLellan, Francois Ponchaud, His Excellency Dr Pen Pannha, Nguyen Tuong Thuy, Gen. (Ret.) Thong Phalla, Trinh Quoc Trong, Uch Arun, and William Townsend (OAM).

A NOTE ON THE PEOPLE REFERRED TO IN THE ENGLISH EDITION

Given below are some of the individuals referred to in this book. In the next two paragraphs, they are listed in order of their appearance in the text.

Heng Samkai was the author's eldest brother, who died after serving as governor of Svay Rieng Province during the 1980s and 1990s. **Heng Tal** was a younger brother killed by the Central Party forces during the Khmer Rouge régime. The late **Samdech Akka Moha Thomak Pothisal Chea Sim** was a co-founding Chairman of the Cambodian People's Party (CPP) and President of the Senate; he passed away in 2015.

Those holding high office at the time of publication of the first Khmer-language edition of this book in 2013 included **Their Excellencies Yi Yon** (Secretary of State at the Ministry of Social Affairs, Veterans and Youth Rehabilitation), **Pol Saroeun** (CPP Standing Committee Member and Commander in Chief of the Royal Cambodian Armed Forces) and **Sim Ka** (CPP Standing Committee Member); **Samdech Vibol Sena Pheakdey Say Chhum** (CPP Deputy

Chairman, Secretary-General of the **CPP Permanent Committee** and President of the Senate), **Samdech Krala Hoam Sar Kheng** (CPP Deputy Chairman, Deputy Prime Minister and Minister of Interior), and **Samdech Akka Moha Sena Padei Techo Hun Sen** (CPP Chairman and Prime Minister); and **Their Excellencies Bou Thong** (CPP Standing Committee Member), **Mean Sam An** (CPP Standing Committee Member and Senator), and the late **Say Phouthang** (CPP Standing Committee Member).

Among the senior Khmer Rouge leaders, former defence minister **Son Sen** died in the Khmer Rouge stronghold of Anlong Veng in 1997. **Pol Pot** died in the same district of Oddar Meanchey Province, in northwest Cambodia, in 1998, paving the way for a definitive end to the civil war at the end of the year. **Ta Mok**, the former head of the Northwestern Zone, was arrested in 1999 and died in custody in 2006 awaiting trial. Former foreign minister **Ieng Sary**, 'Brother Number Two' **Nuon Chea** and former head of state **Khieu Samphan** went on trial at the Extraordinary Chambers in the Courts of Cambodia for crimes against humanity in 2011. **Ieng Sary** died in custody in 2013 as the trial was proceeding. In 2014, **Nuon Chea** and **Khieu Samphan** were convicted of crimes involving the forced evacuation of people from Phnom Penh and other regions and the execution of Lon Nol soldiers immediately after the Khmer Rouge came to power in 1975. They were sentenced to life imprisonment. As this book was going to press, both were still on trial for additional crimes against humanity, grave breaches of the Geneva Conventions of 1949, and genocide against the Muslim Cham and Vietnamese peoples.

CAMBODIAN AND VIETNAMESE MILITARY UNITS

Unit	Cambodian forces	Vietnamese forces*
	People's Revolutionary Army of Kampuchea (1951–1975) Royal Cambodian Armed Forces (1953–1970) Khmer National Armed Forces (1970–1975) National Army of Democratic Kampuchea (1975–1998) People's Revolutionary Armed Forces of Kampuchea (1979–1989) Cambodian People's Armed Forces (1989–1993) Royal Cambodian Armed Forces (1993–present)	People's Liberation Armed Forces of South Vietnam (1961–1976) People's Army of Vietnam (1944–present) ** excludes Army of the Republic of Vietnam*
Division	5,000–10,000	8,000–10,000
Brigade	1,000–1,600	3,500
Regiment	500–1,200	1,500–3,000
Battalion	200–360	300– <1,000
Company	80–120	80–100
Platoon	29–36	29
Group	9–12	9

Note: numbers are approximate and depend on circumstances

INTRODUCTION TO THE ENGLISH EDITION

Among the great guerrilla commanders of the 20th century, the name Heng Samrin is almost unknown. Nevertheless, he went on to be a key player in the foundation of a modern and prosperous Cambodia. Che Guevara and Leon Trotsky lie in their graves revered by the Revolutionary Left but the goals they proclaimed remain as distant as ever. Heng Samrin deserves another look and this autobiography gives us that opportunity. A short, illustrated book, published in 2011, deals with his political campaigns, particularly those following the Vietnamese advance into Cambodia at the end of 1978. This volume focuses on his early life and his role as a military commander working in the eastern region of Cambodia.

This book recounts Heng Samrin's early childhood in a rural village. He was born in 1934, when Cambodia was still part of French Indochina. France had little interest in creating an educated Khmer peasantry and he ultimately fell back on Cambodian tradition, gaining an education when he entered the monkhood at a Buddhist elementary school for five years in 1949.

Following Cambodia's notional independence from France in 1953, he campaigned for the Khmer People's Revolutionary Party in the country's parliamentary elections in 1955. He describes his subsequent work as a rubber plantation worker and farmer before joining the underground Khmer People's Revolutionary Party in 1961. Shortly thereafter, he made his first clandestine contacts with the Viet Cong, the National Liberation Front in Vietnam, the beginning of a relationship that was to serve him well later in his life. As a party member, Heng Samrin worked as a government militia captain and volunteer teacher of village children by day, and as deputy head of an underground courier team by night. After a brutal government crackdown against a rebellion in northwest Cambodia in 1968, he went completely underground.

About this time, he had other encounters that were not so benign. In this book, he gives a vivid first-hand account of airstrikes in the mid-1960s, directed on to his own village by American advisors and the South Vietnamese airforce. Another encounter was with the chimeral Head of State, Prince Norodom Sihanouk, who for a time represented a political challenge to the Khmer People's Revolutionary Party. But puff pieces in the US and French media could not disguise the fact that Sihanouk was essentially a feudal-style prince, albeit an eccentric and charming one, and there was reason to expect that his overthrow in a coup while travelling abroad in 1970 would be the end of his political career. Marshal Lon Nol, the coup leader, declared a republic and then aligned the country with the United States, which was still fighting its war in Vietnam. Prince Sihanouk, in exile in Beijing, aligned his forces with the Khmer People's Revolutionary Party, which he dubbed the *Khmers Rouges*. Working with his former adversaries, the Prince launched the United National Front of Kampuchea to 'liberate' the country and defeat the Lon Nol régime. In the event, Sihanouk commanded few forces of his own and after the capture of Phnom Penh in 1975 would be placed under protective house arrest. From then on, the Prince enjoyed only minor trophy status and his days as a major Cambodian political figure were effectively finished.

Meanwhile, Heng Samrin had begun a meteoric rise in the People's Revolutionary Army of Kampuchea. In five years, he went from section commander to regimental commander, and by 1976 was leading the country's Fourth Division. It was during this period that Cambodia went through one of the greatest political upheavals of the 20th century. However, there were deep political divisions within the revolutionary party, and jubilation was short-lived. Heng Samrin describes conflicts between his own Eastern Zone forces and those from the Southwestern Zone, as the deep shadows of Year Zero spread across the land. He was ordered back to the Eastern Zone after only three months in Phnom Penh.

Heng Samrin recounts how lists of 'traitors' started circulating as early as 1976; and how Pol Pot used a familiar populist ploy, invoking hatred for the Vietnamese, and publicly ordering attacks on Vietnam. The killing of Eastern Zone military commanders and party secretaries followed in 1978 – they were seen not to be enthusiastic enough in carrying out these raids. But not all Khmer Rouge commanders fitted that perception; particular exceptions were those in the Southwestern Zone whose exceptionally savage raids on the Chau Doc and Ha Tien areas inside Vietnam finally caused the Hanoi Politburo's patience to snap. A task force of Cambodian and Vietnamese forces was assembled, and it surged across the border, capturing Phnom Penh in January 1979.

Despite the overthrow of Pol Pot's forces, and notwithstanding the Paris Peace Agreements of 1991 and UN-brokered elections in 1993, a civil war would go on for another two decades. While the remaining Pol Pot forces had made the Thai border area a stronghold, that very situation allowed the Government forces to bottle them up in there. There was no public backing for them within Cambodia, and so they lacked the local support that any guerrilla army needs. Most of Pol Pot's forces had simply died by the turn of the century and, as a political and military entity, they were in no position to impose their ideology on anyone.

Having read the foregoing description, the reader might expect the book, with its emphasis on revolutionary politics, to be a background filler for the 2011 publication. But it offers much more than that. Guerrilla warfare is only dimly understood, even by experts, and Heng Samrin conveys wonderfully that sense of loneliness and isolation that must dog the steps of every intelligent guerrilla during his days in the jungle. The whoosh of fighter bombers overhead, the rattle of gunfire, the thump of distant artillery barrages: what does it mean for you? And this is no idle philosophical rumination – a mistake could cost many lives. 'Being comfortable with ambiguity' is widely recommended by management consultants these days; but in the jungle there is plenty of ambiguity and precious little comfort.

A second, almost quaint, theme that comes through is an obsession with the maintenance of weapons and ammunition, very characteristic of any guerrilla army with access to few workshops and even fewer craftsmen. Weapons are heavy things to carry around all day and they must work whenever and wherever they are needed. Heng Samrin understood this point very well and I suspect he lost hardly any firefights as a result.

The third quality is intuition, a very handy quality when there is not much hard information at hand. Early in the book, Heng Samrin disguises himself to get past hundreds of Khmer Rouge soldiers marching south. He is very matter-of-fact here but as he trudged the remaining few kilometres towards the village where his family had been relocated, he must have wondered what sort of organisation would make such a charade necessary.

The downfall of Lon Nol and the capture of Phnom Penh where his division played a leading role is probably where his doubts hardened into suspicion. Three months after the fall of Phnom Penh, he and his troops were ordered out of the city and back to the Eastern Zone without explanation. The impact of Year Zero was now being felt across the country and the misery from forced evacuations of cities was almost audible. Some other Khmer Rouge military commanders didn't like these policies either but in the case of Heng Samrin, they knew he opposed them – or they thought they did. It didn't matter. He and his troops were to be removed by the centre as soon as possible.

But perhaps his true 'road to Damascus' experience had already come when he was fighting Lon Nol's troops. Back in 1973, one of his units was stricken with malaria and, as there were no medical stocks in hand, one of the staff suggested sending a section to the nearby mountains controlled by the Southwestern Zone to look for traditional medicines and herbs. A section set off for the mountains but never returned. Heng Samrin then sent off a second section armed with letters of introduction and they never returned either. At that point, suspicion would have hardened in to certainty. The governing body of the Cambodian revolution was slowly but surely going insane. It no longer had any claim on his loyalties and one suspects that a cold rage settled in his heart against those who would have his sick soldiers die in such a meaningless way.

The next challenge was not long in coming. Rumours were rife throughout 1977 of a major purge by the *angka* [organisation] of the regional party leadership. When a small mission appeared at his headquarters, inviting Heng Samrin and other local leaders to discussions in Prey Veng, he knew what that really meant. He was not the only one. While most of their colleagues marched off happily to a certain death at the hands of the *angka*, Heng Samrin's colleague So Phim awaited a different fate, killed by Pol Pot forces as he and his family tried to escape to Vietnam. Not so for Heng Samrin who still had many things yet to do. He defected to the Vietnamese with a small group, following in the footsteps of a gangling young man in glasses called Hun Sen. And, as they say, the rest is history.

Two points in conclusion. This is, after all, an autobiography and few authors maul themselves too savagely in such works. But the reader can still make judgments by looking at what authors choose to talk about and what they leave out. Actually, much of the book is occupied by Heng Samrin's soldiers and the Cambodian people, and his deep respect and affection for them is obvious. Cambodia suffered great misfortune in the 20th century. It was very lucky to have men of the calibre of Hun Sen and Heng Samrin to get it out of the pit and to set it on its course to today.

The second point is about guerrilla warfare. It is still with us. Whenever a government becomes too oppressive against its own people, the people always have the mountains and the barrios to fight back from. The quiet footfall in the night, the sudden flash as the local post office bursts into flames – a country can quickly be rendered ungovernable by a clever campaign. Surely it's better to share power with the people while there's still time? It's possible there could be a Heng Samrin in the wings but it's equally likely that there is a Pol Pot. Don't risk it.

Greg Dodds

The writer is a graduate of Australia's Royal Military College at Duntroon in Canberra and served as an Australian Army Intelligence Officer in Vietnam at Nui Dat in 1971. He is now retired and lives in Perth.

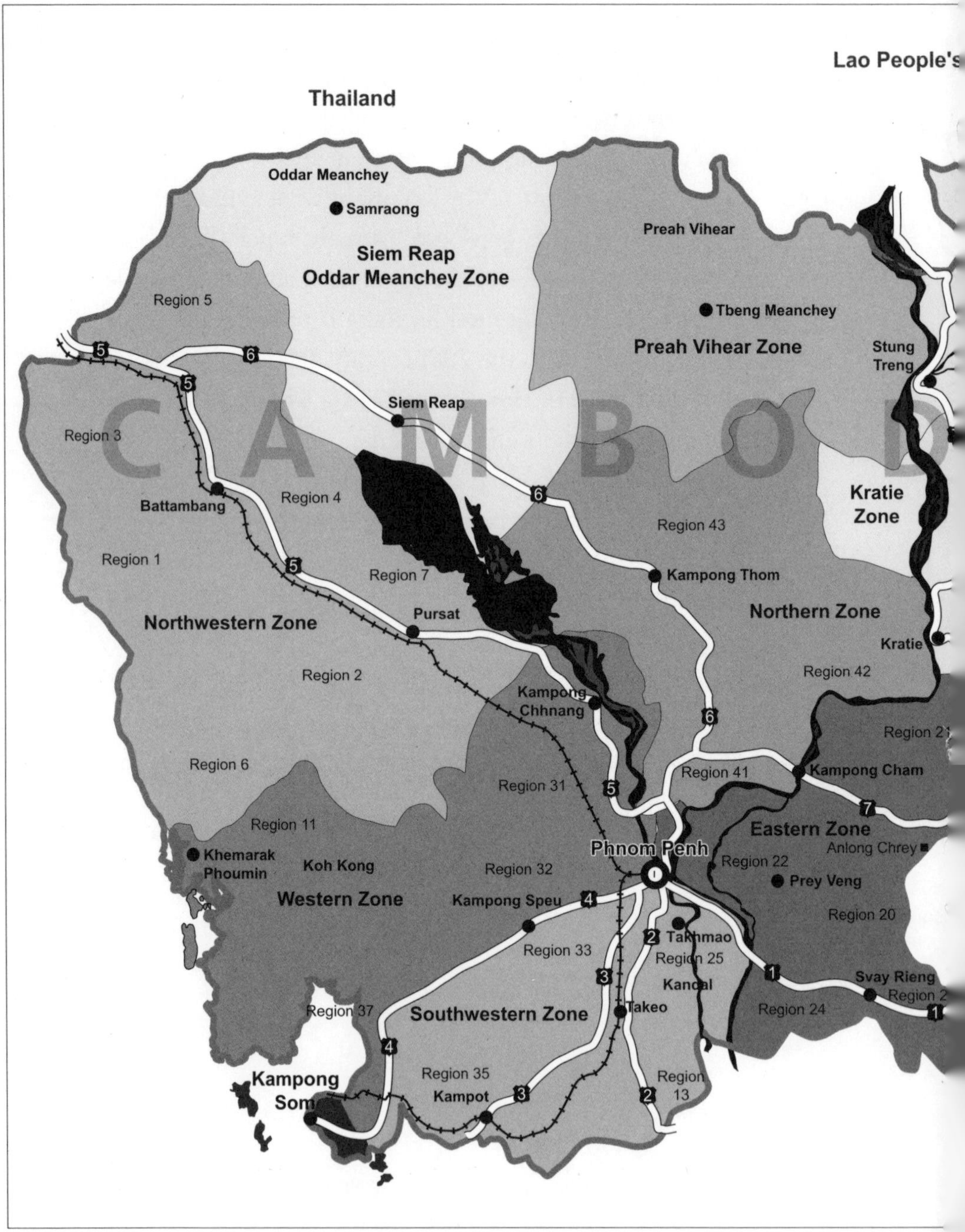
Lao People's
Thailand
Oddar Meanchey
Samraong
Siem Reap
Oddar Meanchey Zone
Preah Vihear
Tbeng Meanchey
Preah Vihear Zone
Stung
Treng
Region 5
CAMBOD
Region 3
Siem Reap
Battambang
Region 4
Kratie
Zone
Region 43
Region 1
Region 7
Kampong Thom
Northern Zone
Pursat
Northwestern Zone
Kratie
Region 2
Region 42
Kampong
Chhnang
Region 21
Region 6
Region 41
Kampong Cham
Region 31
Region 11
Eastern Zone
Anlong Chrey
Khemarak
Phoumin
Koh Kong
Region 32
Phnom Penh
Region 22
Prey Veng
Western Zone
Kampong Speu
Region 20
Takhmao
Region 33
Region 25
Kandal
Svay Rieng
Region 37
Southwestern Zone
Takeo
Region 24
Kampong
Som
Region 35
Kampot
Region
13

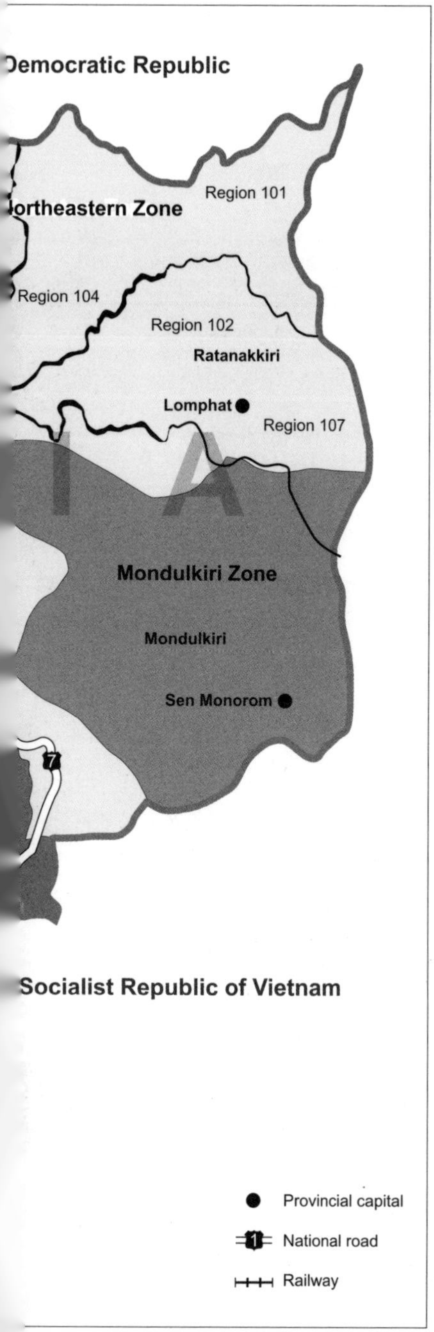

MAP: CHHUT CHHEANA

Cambodia under the Khmer Rouge

Zones and regions under the Khmer Rouge régime (1975–1979). A similar map from the period is on display at the Tuol Sleng Genocide Museum in Phnom Penh. Regions pre-1975 may not correspond exactly.

CHRONOLOGY

1934 Author born in Anlong Chrey Village, Kak Commune, Ponhea Kraek District, Kampong Cham Province (25 May)

1946 Begins studying under assistant abbot of monastery at Wat Trapeang Pring in neighbouring commune of Trapeang Phlong

1949 Enters monkhood at Wat Trapeang Pring; begins five years of study at Buddhist elementary school

1951 Khmer People's Revolutionary Party formed under the leadership of Tou Samouth and Song Ngoc Minh, also known as Achar Mean

1953 Cambodia gains independence from France

1955 Author campaigns for Khmer People's Revolutionary Party in National Assembly elections; later employed as a rubber plantation worker in Kraek

1956 Returns to Anlong Chrey to work as a farmer

1957 Marries Sao Ty in March, and has four children, three girls and a boy: namely Heng Pov, Heng Samaun, Heng Samnang and Heng Samarn

1959 Joins revolutionary movement and becomes involved in Khmer People's Revolutionary Party meetings with National Liberation Front in South Vietnam and agreement to build secret base along border which would later become headquarters for So Phim, commander of the Eastern Zone

1961 Becomes member of Khmer People's Revolutionary Party; later conducts clandestine activities as deputy head of a courier team in the Eastern Zone while holding positions of government militia captain and teacher of village children

1964 Subjected to airstrikes by American and South Vietnamese forces in Anlong Chrey

1966 Eastern Zone border areas attacked as American and South Vietnamese forces begin major military operations against National Liberation Front of Vietnam

1968 Author avoids arrest by government forces after Party urges people to rise up against brutal crackdown; appointed section commander in People's Revolutionary Army of Kampuchea

1969 Appointed director of new field hospital built by So Phim in the village of Samrae in Kak Commune in Ponhea Kraek District; later appointed deputy platoon commander in charge of political affairs

1970 Lon Nol overthrows Prince Norodom Sihanouk in coup d'état; author appointed company commander in People's Revolutionary Army of Kampuchea in the Eastern Zone

1971 Appointed deputy battalion commander of People's Revolutionary Army of Kampuchea

1972 Appointed battalion commander in People's Revolutionary Army of Kampuchea; defeats Lon Nol troops on right bank of Mekong River in Kampong Cham Province in cooperation with Viet Cong Ninth Division

1973 Appointed commander of 126th Regiment of People's Revolutionary Army of Kampuchea with headquarters in O'Reang Ov District in Kampong Cham Province; regiment later redeployed to fight Lon Nol troops in Kandal Province, Prey Veng Province and Svay Rieng Province; conflicts erupt between Eastern Zone forces in Kandal Province and Southwestern Zone forces in Takeo Province

1974 Regiment redeployed to Kandal Province to fight Lon Nol forces on the western side of the Mekong River and along the Bassac River

1975 Enters Phnom Penh from Takhmao as commander of regiment from the Eastern Zone, encounters more tensions with forces from the Southwestern Zone; ordered to withdraw from capital and return to Eastern Zone after three months

1976 Appointed deputy chief of staff of Eastern Zone and Commander of Fourth Division based in Ponhea Kraek District in Kampong Cham Province; responsibilities include guarding and repairing National Road No. 7 and farming to support the unit. Party Centre circulates list of 'traitors' in Eastern Zone

1977 Party announces change of name to Communist Party of Kampuchea and change of founding date; Pol Pot publicly orders armed forces to attack Vietnam

1978 Pol Pot's forces arrest and kill military commanders and Party secretaries in the Eastern Zone; author forms resistance movement with Chea Sim as deputy; seeks assistance from Vietnamese leaders; nominated chairman of the United Front for the National Salvation of Kampuchea; announces 11-point program to overthrow Pol Pot and build a new democratic country (2 December)

1979 Elected to Party Central Committee; assumes chairmanship of provisional government known as the Khmer People's Revolutionary Council a day after Phnom Penh liberated from Pol Pot's forces (7 January)

1981 Elected to National Assembly and Politburo of Khmer People's Revolutionary Party; becomes President of State Council of the People's Republic of Kampuchea and Honorary President of the National Council of the United Front for the Construction and Defence of the Kampuchean Homeland; succeeds Pen Sovann as secretary-general of the Central Committee of the Khmer People's Revolutionary Party

1985 Re-elected secretary-general of the Central Committee; chairs Fifth Party Congress which approves economic reforms and social welfare measures

1989 Chairs meeting which decides to withdraw remaining Vietnamese volunteer troops from Cambodia and adopt policies for private transport and agriculture as well as small industries and handicrafts; meeting also adopts policies on land management, production, natural resources and farm labour; country changes name to State of Cambodia, and forms Supreme National Council with three resistance groups along Thai border

1991 Chairs extraordinary meeting of party which changes name to Cambodian People's Party (CPP), which elects former interior minister Chea Sim party chairman and Prime Minister Hun Sen deputy chairman; elected honorary chairman; State of Cambodia and resistance groups sign Paris Peace Agreements

1993 Elected to National Assembly and appointed Senior Privy Councillor to King Norodom Sihanouk under new constitution for the Kingdom of Cambodia with Funcinpec leader Prince Norodom Ranariddh and Hun Sen as first and second prime ministers

1994 Awarded royal title *Samdech*

1996 Appointed four-star general in the Royal Cambodian Armed Forces

1997 Armed clashes in Phnom Penh between coalition government forces after First Prime Minister Prince Ranariddh seeks to unite his party's forces with Pol Pot's forces; prince flees country; coalition government continues with National Assembly electing Foreign Minister Ung Huot as First Prime Minister

1998 Author elected first vice president of National Assembly with Samdech Hun Sen emerging as sole prime minister; civil war ends with defection of Pol Pot's remaining forces

1999 Cambodia becomes member of the Association of Southeast Asian Nations (ASEAN)

2004 Re-elected first vice president of National Assembly

2006 Elected president of National Assembly, becomes president of National Council of Solidarity Front for Development of the Cambodian Motherland

2007 Awarded royal title *Akka Moha Ponhea Chakrei*

2008 Re-elected president of National Assembly

2009 Appointed five-star general

2010 Assumes presidency of ASEAN Inter-Parliamentary Assembly (AIPA) for one year

2011 Awarded title *Kittipritpandit* by Royal Academy of Cambodia for contributions to the rebirth of the nation, society, tradition and economy as well as humanitarian work

2013 Re-elected president of National Assembly

2015 Assumes two-year presidency of Asian Parliamentary Assembly (APA)

2018 Assumes presidency of Asia-Pacific Parliamentary Forum (APPF)

CHAPTER I

EARLY YEARS

I was born into a poor peasant family in Ponhea Kraek District, in Kampong Cham Province, on 25 May 1934. I was named Heng Him but came to be known by my current name, Heng Samrin, which was shortened to Rin. Until I was 12, I lived with my parents in the village of Anlong Chrey (then known as Anlong Kres) in Kak Commune. In the mornings, the village boys would let cows and buffaloes out of their shelters, leading them to rice paddies near a forest where we tended the animals. In the late afternoons or evenings, we brought the cattle home.

Tending cattle was a typical occupation for country boys, who tried hard to take good care of their animals. In their free time, the boys played Khmer traditional games, *bai khom* and *koun toeung*. The girls also played *bai khom* and another game known as *pok chab*.

Some older people without children also tended cattle. From what I could see, they never wasted time; they did things like string rope, collect firewood and make tethers before rounding up their cattle to come back home. I still remember the thunderstorms in those days, when terrified herders used to run for cover from the rain and lightning.

My chores didn't last long. One day, a monk came to our village to seek alms. Seeing a chance to pursue my dream to study, and without telling my parents, I followed him back to his temple, Wat Thkov, to stay for a day and a night. My parents found out that I was at the temple and came to see me, asking the monk to let me go back home. But they understood my desire for education. Even though they would have to work harder without me, they decided to let me go back to the temple. They bought me a new set of clothes and took me back to the monk, asking him to let me stay so he could teach me and advise me about my future.

During the period when Cambodia was a French protectorate, the authorities generally did not build schools for children to study in villages or communes. Education in rural areas was limited to temples. Wat Thkov had many students but most of them went home in the evening. The facilities were basic. The students sat beneath the monk's house. They had no books. Instead of chalk, the teacher used charcoal. There was no electricity, so to study at night we made a bonfire or used a torch.

I studied at the temple for three months. Fortunately, I met another monk, called Kong So, who was first assistant abbot at a monastery in the village of Trapeang Pring, Trapeang Phlong commune. He came to Wat Thkov during Buddhist Lent. When the rainy-season retreat came to an end, he returned to his temple in Trapeang Phlong. Wanting to study under the Venerable Kong So, I followed him there along with two friends, Ith Aum (Lai) and Mer Moch. After about a year, both of them decided to return to their village because they missed their homes and families. I also missed my family, but I was determined to keep studying and serving the monk, in order to better myself. The Venerable Kong So was delighted and paid more attention to my studies. He was like a parent. I stayed with him until 1949 when I myself became a monk, studying at a Buddhist elementary school for five years. I left the monkhood in 1954.

I went back to my village. Under the leadership of Prince Norodom Sihanouk, elections for the National Assembly were held in 1955. Several political parties took part, including the Sangkum Reastr Niyum, the Khmer People's Revolutionary Party and the Democratic Party. Independence from France having been won in 1953, this was a very important political event for Cambodia. I liked the Khmer People's Revolutionary Party, so I decided to campaign actively for them during the election. So Phai was the Party's representative in the Kampong Cham constituency and he worked very hard with Party members and supporters.

However, the Sangkum Reastr Niyum won a resounding victory. One factor in their success may have been the conclusions of the Geneva Conference of 1954, convened to resolve a number of issues in the aftermath of the Korean War (1950–53) and the First Indochina War (1946–54). This led to the dispersal of the forces of the Revolutionary Party, and a loss of public support. Furthermore, most people maintained their faith in the monarchy.*

After the election, I went back to work as a farmer. Soon I was hired to work at a rubber plantation in Kraek where I was joined by

---

* EDITOR'S NOTE: *According to American historian Robert Randle's account of the conference published in 1969, Vietnamese Prime Minister Pham Van Dong proposed that both the Khmer Issarak and Pathet Lao resistance governments be represented at the Geneva Conference, a proposal supported by Soviet Foreign Minister Vyacheslev Molotov but rejected by Cambodian delegation leader Sam Sary, who described the Khmer Issarak as 'foreigners who are being manipulated by a foreign bloc.' US Under Secretary of State Walter Bedell Smith dismissed the Khmer and Lao resistance forces as 'so-called governments' that did not qualify for invitations to the conference. Australian journalist Wilfred Burchett later wrote that the consequences of the 1954 conference were a 'major impediment to the Cambodian revolution' and that the Khmer resistance fighters were 'robbed at Geneva of their share of the fruits of the common victory by the three peoples of Indochina over French colonialism'.*

a number of poor workers from different places. During the French colonial period, rubber was mostly planted in Kampong Cham Province where the fertile soil has a distinct red colour. The French introduced the rubber trees in places such as Kraek, Chub, Memot, Stueng Trang and Chamkar Leu. The number of leaves determined a tree's value – more leaves meant more money. Rubber seemed to promise huge profits.

New workers at the plantation earned 25 riel a day and had to work eight or more hours under the strict supervision of the owner or a foreman. It was difficult working there as it was my first job, away from home and family, and I couldn't handle my duties well. At the same time, I was now a working man, no longer a youth. Before going to bed, I used to question in my mind the development prospects for this new nation, just freed from French colonial rule. It was so weak. What was my future going to be? Despite my exhaustion after work, these thoughts went round and round in my head, and made it hard for me to fall asleep at night.

After spending a short time as a worker, I decided to return home, and in March 1957, I got married. My wife is Sao Tieb, also known as Sao Ty (we now have three daughters and a son). We lived together on our farm and worked hard. For farmers on the plain, growing sugar palm trees, the work was very arduous, especially in the dry season. In their spare time, they cut bark from the palm trees to string rope or make tethers for their cattle. To earn money for family expenses, they could sell what they didn't need for themselves. The situation of farmers living near the forest was much easier. In both the dry and wet seasons, they could go into the forest whenever they were free to collect vines and rattan, or cut down trees to make ploughs and harrows.

During my spare time in the dry season, I would string as much rope as possible for my family. The surplus was sold to other farmers.

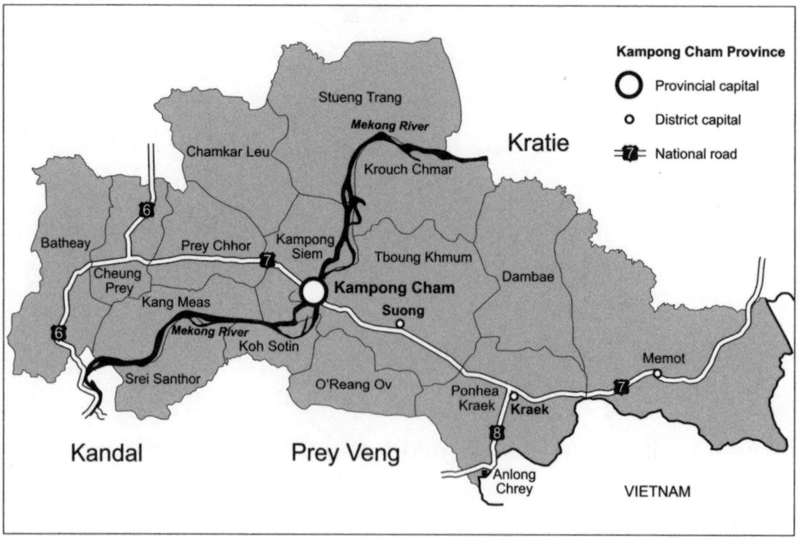

MAP: CHHUT CHHEANA

Kampong Cham Province

Wearing shorts, a long black shirt and a palm-leaf hat, I used to ride an old bicycle with bunches of carefully tied rope on the luggage rack.

When the wet season came, I tried to follow the example of other farmers in the village by working faster. When there was enough rain, farming generally yielded good produce for farmers and their living standards were better. But if there was a drought, yields were poor and they would always run out of food the next year. To make ends meet, farmers had to earn as much as possible during their free time. Otherwise, they could end up borrowing rice from other people to meet their basic needs.

CHAPTER 2

JOINING THE REVOLUTION

It was during 1959, when I was living with my family and working to support them, that a representative of the Khmer People's Revolutionary Party visited our village. His name was Sok. He was a former Khmer Issarak leader who also went by the name of Monobramkhet. He met privately with my cousin Chakk Yann and me. He wanted to go to Vietnam to talk with representatives of the National Liberation Front of South Vietnam (Viet Cong) and asked me to find a secret route across the border. This proposal chimed in with our own political inclinations. We seized the opportunity. Following a confidential discussion on how to make contact in Vietnam, we left the village at dawn the next day with a long-handled machete, a cooking pot with some rice and other food for the journey.

At that time, war was raging in the southern part of Vietnam. The resistance forces of the National Liberation Front had a base in Tay Ninh Province in South Vietnam, which bordered Prey Sandann, Prey Traeng and Otakoun in Cambodia. These forces were being heavily attacked by American and South Vietnamese forces. At dusk, we reached an old Khmer temple called Wat Tnaot, built during the French colonial period. It was located in a remote area and abandoned. Knowing that the National Liberation Front often patrolled and stayed in the area, Chakk Yann, Sok and I waited for three days before finally meeting them. Sok could speak Vietnamese fluently. It was the first such meeting, from what I could tell, and it went on a long time. The main purpose was for us to get to know one another and have a general discussion about our earlier joint resistance to colonial forces in Cambodia, Vietnam and Laos. At the end of the meeting, we said goodbye, promising to report the outcome to our respective leaders, and meet again.

Five days later, a second meeting was held at another location, called Khnach Tachey, which was more secure. The Vietnamese side acknowledged the rôle of our resistance forces and agreed to build a base next to the border which would be protected by five Vietnamese guards. We all agreed to support each other at all times. The base was to be in Ta Am, a village in the eastern part of Thlok Trach Commune. It would later become a top-secret base for quarterly meetings of the Khmer People's Revolutionary Party Centre. Sok supervised the base with So Phim, who was in charge of the whole of the Eastern Zone for the revolutionary forces. So Phim, also known as Sovanna, later developed a clear structure, including a regional department led by a man called Bai. He was succeeded by Soy Sisaphon, a regional representative also known as Phoung who explained revolutionary theory to me.

I was enthusiastic about the theory. I tried very hard, emotionally and physically, to carry out my duties for the Khmer People's Revolutionary Party. In 1961, my wife and I were both accepted to be Party members on the recommendation of Bai and Sok, seconded by Phoung. My superiors in the Party hierarchy – Ith Aum, So Heng (Sam) and my cousin Ek Suth – instructed me to attend all meetings at the Party's regional branch office, which was directly supervised by Bai.

As part of our covert operations in the region, I was named deputy head of the courier team for the Eastern Zone, which was led by Ith Aum. Other members of the team were Khao Sam, my older brother Heng Samkai, and my younger brother Heng Tal along with Heng Lim and Ek Suth. We came under the direct command of So Phim, whose responsibilities included bringing Party officials from other zones to the Eastern Zone and sometimes carrying secret Party messages from the Eastern Zone to Phnom Penh or other zones.

While carrying out clandestine activities for the party, I was also serving as a captain in the government militia and as a volunteer teacher of village children. Therefore I was above suspicion. I could move back and forth quite easily. In my position, I urged people to set up legal associations for cultivating and ploughing fields and transplanting seedlings, for holding funerals and weddings, and also for young people and sports. These could help relieve some of the hardships experienced by the villagers of Anlong Chrey, who were extremely poor and suffered great shortages. My clandestine activities went smoothly, so I was constantly praised by my superiors.

By then, the situation along the border was serious. Americans and their South Vietnamese allies were launching airstrikes on Vietnamese territory near the Cambodian border, causing damage and creating difficulties for the National Liberation Front. The Viet Cong took shelter along the border, and were sometimes forced to enter Cambodia temporarily, waiting for things to improve in Vietnam.

In this intense environment along the border, Cambodian government forces were well prepared. One day in 1964, American and South Vietnamese warplanes bombarded Anlong Chrey. It was around 5:30 p.m. As the sun was setting and people were returning from work, herding cattle into their shelters, the aircraft struck our village. Afterwards, there was a moment of silence. Then I could see many houses engulfed in flames or damaged by fallen trees. I could hear people groaning. It was getting dark so the search for victims was extremely difficult, and we were afraid of unexploded bombs. There were hospitals in the towns of Suong and Kampong Cham but the road was narrow and difficult to travel. Around 10:00 p.m. that evening, a group of private doctors arrived from the French rubber plantation at Kraek. They treated the wounded till morning, when district and provincial officials arrived with government troops. Many were equipped with heavy weapons and handguns.

At least 12 people were killed and many others injured in this first airstrike on Anlong Chrey by American and South Vietnamese forces. Houses were destroyed and a lot of cattle, pigs, chickens and ducks killed. Around 9:00 the next morning, a second strike came. The village was still in chaos as the Americans and South Vietnamese flew over in six helicopters and several planes, firing shots and dropping bombs. Numerous government soldiers were killed or injured. Only a metre from the trench where I was sheltering, a coconut tree was hit by a rocket and exploded into pieces. When I ran for safety, a government soldier accused me of deserting my base, threatening to open fire.

At the time, I had orders to welcome senior Khmer People's Revolutionary Party officials from Phnom Penh and other regions for an annual meeting at our base along the border at Thlok Trach. But following the attacks, the meeting was postponed. After the initial strikes, the helicopters of the American and South Vietnamese forces patrolled both day and night around Anlong Chrey. Life was very difficult. People used to run to the revolutionary base from their homes, seeking shelter under distant trees along the edge of a canal to the west of the paddy fields. They were afraid of gathering in groups. Farming was done only at night since people were frightened of being seen and shot by the Americans and their allies in Saigon.

In 1966, American and South Vietnamese forces launched Operation Attleboro, which was followed by Operation Junction City. These operations were overseen by Robert McNamara, a former air force lieutenant-colonel who was the American Defense Secretary at the time. In Cambodia, the fighting took place along the border from the area around Xa Mat checkpoint to Trapeang Phlong and to the south of Kampong Meanchey, the village next to Thlok Trach. The action involved warplanes, an armoured division, and artillery. It lasted several days and nights and was especially intense around Kampong Meanchey. The deadliest clashes involved troops of the National Liberation Front. They fought for three days and three nights to inflict a humiliating defeat on the American and South Vietnamese troops, who withdrew.

In Cambodia, government forces were later used to suppress unrest that followed popular uprisings in Samlout in Battambang Province, Kampong Thom Province and other parts of the country. Facing a widespread rebellion by crowds demanding solutions to a number of problems, government forces launched a deadly crackdown in Phnom Penh and other places such as Sre Chipov, Sre Or, Pong Cha, Boeung Khtom, Chamlong Korng, Chi Sang, Kampong Kul and Kror Nhung. About 2,000 people were killed and many others injured. Many villages and communes were destroyed, along with revolutionary bases.

The crackdown devastated the revolutionary movement. Many people, including party cadres, lost faith in the struggle. Our forces dared not operate openly and went underground. Many cadres escaped to the Eastern Zone and other parts of the country to resume their activities. Weapons were being confiscated. The crackdown was brutal in every part of the country except the area I controlled. The last holdout was Anlong Chrey, where three farmers were killed and several houses and all of the people's barns, including ours, were burned down. Some of us escaped into the forest.

On 20 August 1968, the Central Committee of the Khmer People's Revolutionary Party issued a declaration, calling on people across the country to stand up, and carry out a political and military uprising against the crackdown in which innocent people were being arrested and killed by the armed forces. In an effort to wipe out the revolutionary movement, and given that the Eastern Zone was considered our stronghold, government forces constantly surrounded us, carrying out arrests and killings.

In addition to the American and South Vietnamese bombings, people in Anlong Chrey and many other villages and communes were being attacked and killed by our own government forces. When weapons were confiscated from our government militia at Ta Haev District, I fled to the forest near the village to monitor the situation. Three days later, I saw three trucks with about 40 soldiers surrounding the village, and my house in particular. They were looking for me. 'Where is your husband?' they asked my horrified wife. She replied: 'He received a letter from the District and went there three days ago but hasn't come back.'

They soon disappeared but returned about five days later, surrounding the village again. I observed more soldiers this time. Upon entering the village, they burned down houses and barns. After retreating, they sent 10 armed soldiers back to the village. But this third attempt also failed – I was on the alert and they did not find me. However, they did arrest four men – Kao Nhung, the eldest; Preab Chun; a 17-year-old called Thim Phon; and my cousin's son Phy, whose real name was Eang Paek. Phy managed to escape. The three others were shot dead and buried in a pit.

I was hiding in the forest to the east of the village with So Suk (also known as Keo Sin, who after Liberation in 1979 became the Governor of Kampong Chhnang Province). After hearing gunshots, we went to assess the situation. Each of us had weapons and some medical gear. It was around 5:30 p.m. and we were ready to attack the enemy around Tuol Village (where Anlong Chrey Reservoir is now located). However, the soldiers left from the western side of the village and headed from Chas Kak Lich Village to Ta Am Village via Wat Thkov.

The people of Anlong Chrey, Bos Ampel and other nearby villages could no longer bear to live in such a state of suffering, and escaped back into the forest. They had no food, water, shelter or medicine. They had no alternative but to endure the hardship. Later, I discussed with some village elders how people might be persuaded to return home, although young men of around 17 or 18 had to remain hidden, as they were the main targets of government forces.

To control the people of Anlong Chrey and nearby villages, the authorities set up camps and rounded people up, especially families suspected of being sympathetic to the revolutionary movement. The situation was very tense. To block supplies reaching the revolutionary forces in the forest, soldiers were assigned every day to watch families whose members had escaped. There were constant arrests and killings in villages such as Ampil, Santey, Ponley, Trapeang Stieng, Bos Ti, Kanhchae, Dang Kdaong, Phum Bos and Bos Roka. Several people were killed at Dauntei Reservoir. Across the border in Prey Veng Province, others from Kanlaeng Chroau Village in Krabao Commune in Kamchay Mear District were arrested and brutally killed at Oprich.

With our revolutionary forces ravaged by government troops,

the Eastern Zone established a company with Chan Samorn as commander and Heng Tal, my younger brother, as his deputy. A platoon was also set up with guards and intelligence agents divided into six units, covering 20 regions including Region 5, which was Ponhea Kraek District (previously Ta Haev District). In the province of Prey Veng, Region 10 was Kamchay Mear District and Region 12 was Kanhchriech District. There were also several mobile units to carry out activities north of National Road No. 7.

I was given the role of deputy leader of a special technical courier team. I worked at various bases, keeping in touch with core forces in villages such as Ponley, Trapeang Stieng, Phum Bos, Bos Roka, Reul and Dauntei in Ponhea Kraek District as well as Trapeang Banteay in Romeas Haek District in Svay Rieng Province.

Once, I witnessed a terrible incident when government troops arrested a man at Kandaol Chrum Market. Born in Ponley, Ta Muon had been a revolutionary in the area north of National Road No. 7. Shackled with chains running from his neck to his ankles, he was forced to walk, tortured, and accused of being a communist. He was then grabbed and taken into the forest, and disembowelled in Trapeang Phlong. By coincidence, the troops came into the area where my unit of eight men was sitting in a circle in camouflage. It was around 9:00 a.m. and I was lying on a rattan hammock; old ladies from the village were bringing us food. Then we heard some noise. I stood up and looked behind me, and saw soldiers about five metres away. I yelled at my men to open fire but they missed their targets. I shouted for them to keep shooting. The government soldiers panicked and tried to hide, so we withdrew from the forest. After running about 100 metres, the soldiers started firing 60mm shells at the spot where we had just been. We walked through bushes in Trapeang Touk Field before reaching the paddy fields. It was the rice-planting season, so we disguised ourselves as farmers. The soldiers did not return to the Kraek military camp until the afternoon.

Until early 1969, there were frequent clashes with government soldiers. So Phim, the commander of the Eastern Zone, built a field hospital in the southern part of the forest in Samrae Village to treat the sick and injured. I was assigned to run the hospital and tried to provide treatment to the wounded and disabled. The situation in the region then started to improve.

So Phim later sent me to the platoon in Section Six of Region 20, to move deeper into the districts of Ponhea Kraek as well as Kamchay Mear and Kanhchriech in Prey Veng. During an operation in Kamchay Mear, we camped in the forest on the southwest shore of a lake, Boeung Phnos Doun Mao, which was to the east of a village called Cheach. While we were stationed in this area, there was a firefight in which government soldiers were killed and injured. On our side, one of our soldiers called Sarun was seriously wounded in the hip, but he was strong and looked fine. After the fighting, we remained on the alert. Since the area bordered Vietnam, some of our forces crossed into Vietnam and others escaped to villages along the border.

When they returned, they brought rice wine. Reaching the site of the recent fighting, we sat and drank – and heard the sound of a voice wailing. We thought it was a ghost. Someone poured a few drops of liquor on the ground and said: 'Sarun, please drink this wine that I'm pouring for you now.' But we could still hear the voice, so we all went to where it was coming from. We found Sarun hiding in a hole in the trunk of a tree. We dragged him out and carried him to our base for emergency treatment. At the medical facility, I gave him first aid. He was then sent to our field hospital in Samrae for further treatment. (Later, after 1979, Sarun became Governor of Kampong Speu Province. At the time of writing, he lives in the village of Trapeang Krasang in Cheach Commune in Kamchay Mear District, in Prey Veng.)

By this time, I was a deputy platoon commander in charge of political affairs in Section Six. Sarun, whose nickname was Ta Sror Morm ('Bearded Grandpa'), was a deputy platoon commander in charge of general affairs in the same section. The number of soldiers increased to 60 and their duties included protecting politicians visiting villages for propaganda purposes. The propaganda activities were shared, with Khim (Suon) and Chamroeurn working in Doun Daok, Kong Sakun in Tuol Sangkae, and Ros Pos Pi, Ta Krohorm and Tasung in other villages.

In 1970, Prime Minister and former chief of the the armed forces Lon Nol and his group overthrew Chief of State Prince Sihanouk in a coup d'état. Cambodia was entering a new era.

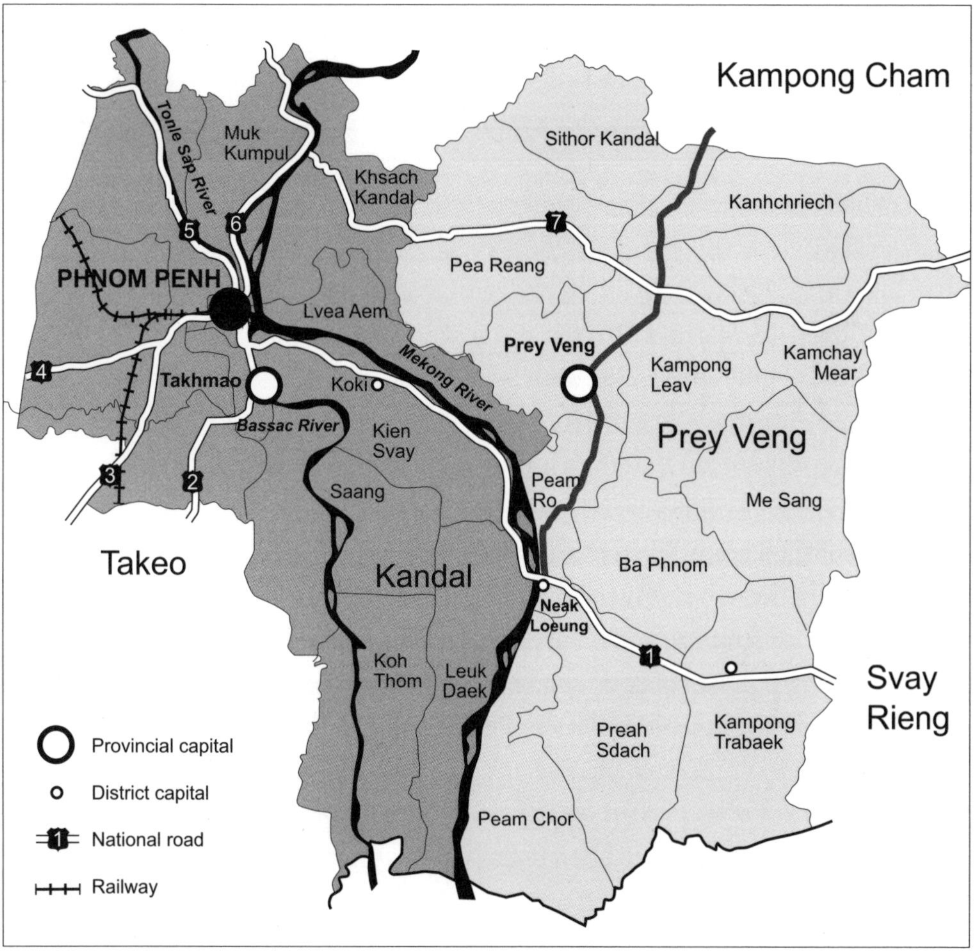

MAP: CHHUT CHHEANA

Prey Veng and Kandal Provinces

CHAPTER 3

FALSE DAWN

On 18 March 1970, the prime minister Marshal Lon Nol, his deputy Prince Sisowath Sirik Matak and their political allies overthrew Prince Norodom Sihanouk in a coup d'état. The prince was abroad, leading a top-level delegation seeking aid to solve the country's economic crisis. Lon Nol abolished the monarchy and established a pro-Western Khmer Republic.

After the coup, Prince Sihanouk and his delegation went to Beijing. With support from China, he issued a statement on 23 March accusing Lon Nol of conducting an illegitimate coup and calling for the new government in Phnom Penh to be overthrown. The prince condemned American interference in Cambodia as well as Vietnam and Laos. He also called for the establishment of a United National Front of Kampuchea to liberate Cambodia, dissolve the government and parliament of Lon Nol, and build Cambodia 'with independence, peace, neutrality, non-alliance and prosperity'.

After hearing the prince's announcement from Beijing, Cambodians across the country rose up in protest against the coup. In the Eastern Zone, there were riots in villages such as Anlong Chrey, which was close to the government military camps of Angkaeng and Khna on National Road No. 7. Lon Nol's officials and soldiers went on a rampage, shooting and arresting people. Many protestors were killed and injured. Our forces came out of the forests to welcome the popular uprising and help people fight, surrounding the Angkaeng camp for three days and three nights. We helped remove the dead and take the injured to our field hospital in Samrae. Yet the protestors and our forces could not destroy the camp, which received support from government forces at the main camp in Prey Veng at Krabao, in Kamchay Mear District. The government forces attacked from the air, and dispersed the crowds of people by force before regrouping at Krabao camp.

Rioting spread through the Eastern Zone and elsewhere across the nation. My unit and others which were camping in the forest moved further from the village of Pratheat on National Road No. 7 to the communes of Chak Chruol and Damril in O'Reang Ov District.

With support from the Americans and their South Vietnamese allies, Lon Nol's forces set up two main camps at Krabao and Kraek in the Eastern Zone. By helicopter, they transported to the camps more troops and weapons from Phnom Penh and Saigon, including 105mm cannons, in preparation for battle. Our forces called an urgent meeting and formulated plans to attack them in advance, before they could reinforce the camps. A nearby division of the National Liberation Front of South Vietnam cooperated with my unit and we monitored the area, planning our attack for the next full moon. The Viet Cong division and our unit decided that the attack could not be delayed.

With good intelligence on the enemy bases, my unit and the Viet Cong division launched a major offensive against the Lon Nol camps. We destroyed the entire camp at Krabao, capturing many prisoners and confiscating thousands of handguns and heavy weapons. Soldiers who could escape fled to the town of Prey Veng. The Lon Nol forces suffered heavy losses as the revolutionary forces continued their offensive, liberating numerous districts such as Kamchay Mear and Kanhchriech in Prey Veng and Romeas Haek in Svay Rieng.

On the same night, in Kampong Cham, our troops attacked the camp in Kraek. Initially we could not defeat the government forces there as we had no field intelligence, but we continued fighting for another three days and three nights. Finally we destroyed and captured the base, taking over districts such as Ponhea Kraek, Tboung Khmum, O'Reang Ov, Krouch Chhmar and Memot. In Kratie Province, the districts of Snuol and Chhlong were also liberated, and eventually the whole province.

With the country heading towards war, So Phim, with the support of Viet Cong forces, set up a military training base in Serei Au in Romeas Haek District in Svay Rieng. He formed a joint committee led by Reach Phorn, who was under orders to identify experienced former soldiers from the region who could command patrols, platoons or companies, and make arrangements for full complements of young soldiers in each unit. The committee then formed ten companies and I was promoted to command a battalion.

Assembling these soldiers was easy – people were suffering, and furious with Lon Nol and his supporters for overthrowing Prince Sihanouk. In addition, they were responding to appeals by the exiled prince for the resistance forces to flee to the maquis forest and rise up against the coup.

After we gathered the soldiers as planned, we started training them in fighting techniques and skills. At the closing ceremony for the first training course, So Phim urged them to make every effort to gain victory over the enemy in the causes of national independence, freedom and rights for the people, and economic development. Under an order issued after the ceremony, three battalions headed north to Kampong Cham. Tal commanded the first battalion, I led the second and Tat the third.

My unit left for Kampong Cham. We camped in the forest to the west of the village of Santey Lich and to the east of the villages of Dang Kdaong, Kanhchae, Trapeang Stieng and Ponley. It was here that my unit conducted strategic military training. The Americans and their South Vietnamese allies dispatched infantry, armoured tanks and artillery units to National Road No. 7, through the Xa Mat-Trapeang Phlong border checkpoint in Kampong Cham Province. They also passed through checkpoints in Bavet District in Svay Rieng Province, to National Road No. 1, and Troeung in Snuol District in Kratie Province. They advanced to Suong town and the Chub rubber factory in Tboung Khmum District. The fighting was heavy. They bombed Suong Market, the rubber factory and a paper mill in Chhlong District in Kratie Province. They conducted a large-scale operation day and night to link the zones where they were dominant, Kampong Cham and Phnom Penh. However, forces backing Lon Nol and Sirik Matak officials were being defeated in most places across the country.

The combat was intense. The enemy had aircraft cover, armour and artillery. But our forces were spreading out from the border, attacking them and defeating them with relative ease. The government forces abandoned their garrisons along National Road No. 7, such as Chong Angkrang Khna, Kandaol Chrum, Bat Lea, Kraek, Ampuk, Saam, Preah Phdauv and Trapeang Phlong.

I mobilised the 300 soldiers under my command to take action in Svay Antor District in Prey Veng Province, based in several villages including Prey Russei, Prey Khla and Prey Voar and Svay Antor. We were under the command of the Viet Cong Ninth Division. They provided us with military assistance, logistics and our daily living needs; we were in charge of our administration and made our own political decisions.

While stationed here, my unit regularly trained in military tactics. From 1972, it was restructured as the Twelfth Battalion and camped near Tnaut Village, Kanhchriech District. As our battalion grew in size, we separated from the Viet Cong Ninth Division and kept only five Vietnamese advisors.

In this new battalion, we had three commanders. Two had just come back from studying in North Vietnam – Keo Chuon was chief of military affairs and Reach Sambath was head of political affairs. As a local cadre, I was the third commander and served as deputy chief of both military and political affairs. Pin was chief of general staff. After this structure was set up, we trained in military techniques, political theory and ideology for a month before leaving Tnaut for Koh Sotin District in Kampong Cham. We camped in Moha Khnhoung commune, in the villages of Khnhoung Leu and Mohasiek. From here, we attacked Lon Nol's troops on the right bank of the Mekong River in Kang Meas District and, with the support of the Viet Cong Seventh Division, overran Lon Nol's camp at Peam Chikong. We later attacked a military base defending Ou Chleung Bridge and captured a lieutenant commander, liberating the whole area. Our forces occupied the area for some time just in case Lon Nol's troops, with back-up from the town of Kampong Cham, counter-attacked at Prek Deumchan Bridge in Kampong Siem District (between the islands of Koh Prak and Koh Kul). I still remember Lon Nol's forces being under the command of In Tam, who was giving orders from the air. His soldiers ruthlessly destroyed everything in their path, but could not hold their positions. Finally, they were forced to withdraw to the provincial capital of Kampong Cham.

At that time, conflicts erupted between revolutionary forces in the

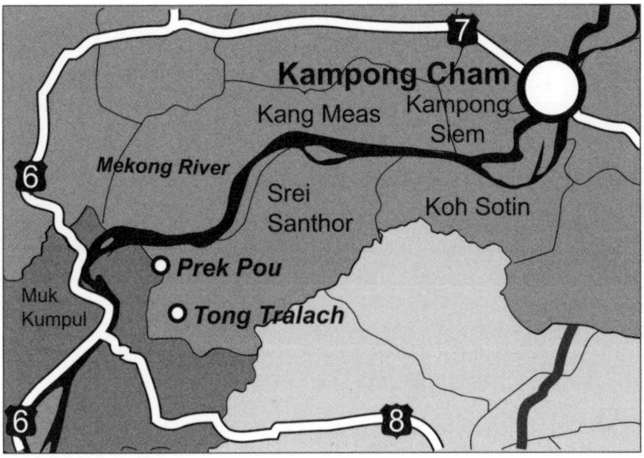

MAP: CHHUT CHHEANA

Battlefields in Kampong Cham and Kandal Provinces

Eastern Zone and the Northern Zone, especially Region 31 (later part of the Western Zone). Northern forces accused us of using their territory to attack the enemy, confiscating our weapons. I travelled to Region 31 to solve the problem with Sreng, the Northern Zone commander.

The Eastern Zone later ordered my unit into action across the Mekong River on the left bank. After getting our orders, we camped in Prek Pou in Srei Santhor District and conducted operations as far as Preah Prasap, Preah Konglong Bridge, Prek Ta Meak, Tong Tralach and Khna Sar villages, reaching Muk Kumpul District in Kandal Province. In Muk Kumpul, we attacked and destroyed a garrison stationed on Bak Kaeng Bridge. We confiscated numerous weapons and explosives and then crossed the river back to Prek Pou with a three-year-old girl whose parents were killed during the attack. She was taken care of, and brought up by Ta Tum, a secretary of Region 22.

In 1973, the Eastern Zone promoted me to command the 126th Regiment which comprised three battalions – the Twelfth, the Sixteenth and the Seventeenth. I regularly trained them in O'Reang Ov District to be prepared for battle. We built the regimental headquarters near Prasat Village in Chak Chruol Commune, O'Reang Ov, Kampong Cham Province.

Six months later, the Eastern Zone ordered us into action on the west (right) bank of the Mekong River (Region 25). This region extended along the Bassac River and covered four districts, namely Kien Svay, Saang, Koh Thom and Leuk Daek in Kandal Province. We knew Lon Nol's troops still occupied some posts in the area. So before mobilising all our forces, I dispatched some to attack these remaining posts, especially those in Peam Ro District in Prey Veng. It did not take them long to secure these positions. Then we crossed the Mekong River to take control of National Road No. 1 from Kampong Phnom Krao to Prek Pol, Banteay Daek and Khsom. We occupied these positions and then withdrew some of our forces from National Road No. 1 to camp along the Bassac River in the villages of Ta You Prasat, Prek Russei, Prek Slaeng and Tuol Speu as well as Ta Khlork Market. To combat infiltrators, we allocated some of our forces to work with village militia in conducting guerrilla attacks.

In Saang District, I built a field hospital at Prek Slaeng for the sick and wounded. The hospital was our logistics base for all units camped in the area. I then planned to attack a garrison in Kampong Svay next to Wat Doung, by the main road to Sre Ampel Monastery. Since Lon Nol's troops were well fortified, it took us three nights to attack and take control.

Along the Mekong River, I ordered my forces to string metal cables across the water to trap vessels transporting all kinds of weapons and foodstuffs to Lon Nol's officials in Phnom Penh. Our forces destroyed many naval vessels and large ships including one with 155mm artillery and thousands of tonnes of explosives which sank around the island of Koh Tachou. We also sank a vessel trying to disguise itself with a Soviet flag around Sarikakeo. We captured another ship carrying explosives. We boarded it and confiscated all the explosives. During the wet season of 1973, the Mekong River flooded across lakes and lowlands, but not across the higher ground or National Road No.1. I found the situation increasingly difficult, so I commanded my forces to withdraw temporarily from the battlefield along the national road.

By PC-25 field radio, I heard about bombings by B-52 aircraft along National Road No. 1. The bombed area was around Deumchrey and the Ong Ko Catholic Church, on the western side of the road, and around mango plantations and a cattle shed on the eastern side as far as Wat Koki Thom and Wat Prek Thmei. I heard by radio that they would bomb our area soon, so I ordered all my forces to leave by 2:00 p.m. At around 5:30 p.m., three B-52 aircraft bombed the area. Since they were far from the trenches, some of our soldiers were killed and others wounded. One of the dead soldiers was called Rin, the same name as mine. We carried the dead and wounded back to Ta You Prasat on a horse-drawn cart and some makeshift stretchers, especially those who could not be treated at the site. Some of the dead were buried at Prek Slaeng in Ta Lon Commune in Saang District; other dead and wounded were taken to Kien Svay District.

Hearing of the death of my namesake, my family thought I was dead and began grieving, even though my unit told them that I was alive and that it was another Rin who was killed. My family did not believe So Phim, so he ordered me to go home to let my wife and children see me in person. I went home straight away so they could see me with their own eyes. I spent a few days with my family in the village and then went back to the unit.

The situation in Phnom Penh was tense. The revolutionary forces were surrounding the capital and had built camps close to the city. The battlefield was to the east of Phnom Penh, along the Bassac

River, including the districts of Leuk Daek, Koh Thom, Saang and Kien Svay. We had three regiments – the 173rd commanded by Chan Chakrey, the 126th by me, and the 160th by Soung – stationed ready for attack as soon as we received orders. Chan Chakrey was the front-line commander and I was his deputy. My regiment was positioned in the villages of Kien Svay and conducting operations from Ta You Prasat, Prek Russei and Prek Slaeng to Prek Pra Monastery, Doun Sar and especially the Roboah Angkanh area.

After taking up our positions, we received orders from the Eastern Zone to attack a military post at Angkor Chey in a joint operation with forces of the Southwestern Zone. They were stationed in a village next to Phnom Chiso, a mountain in the southeast of Prey Kabass District in Takeo Province. Under the plan, the 126th Regiment was to fight for the Angkor Chey base while the 173rd Regiment would counter any enemy attacks from Phnom Penh, either by National Road No. 1 or by the Mekong River around Sdau Khsom Village.

It was the wet season, and attacks on enemy positions took place as river waters were rising. To go into battle, we used boats and either swam or floated across the water holding on to the trunks of banana trees. The attack on Angkor Chey started at around 2:00 a.m. It lasted until 7:00 a.m. when I suddenly saw enemy tanks from Dei Edth coming to the aid of the post. They were attacking us from behind. Our forces fought back but were disorganised. Twenty of our men in the mortar platoon were captured and imprisoned in Phnom Penh (until 17 April 1975, when I had them freed and returned to our regiment). To determine our points of strength and weakness, all units were called to a meeting so we could revise our plans for the next fight. Soon after the meeting, the flood waters were reaching a critical level.

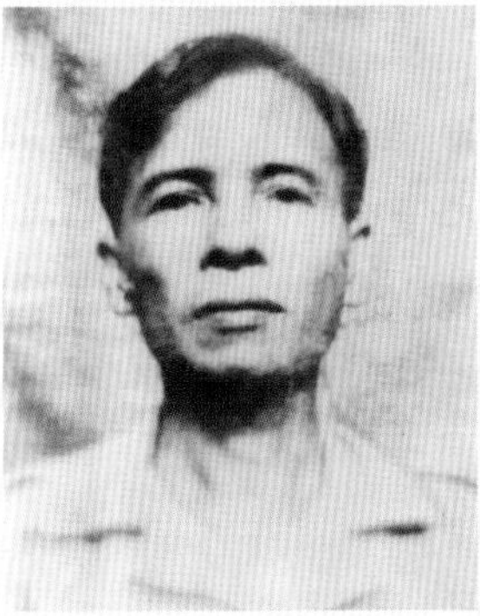

Tou Samouth,
Secretary-General, Khmer People's Revolutionary Party

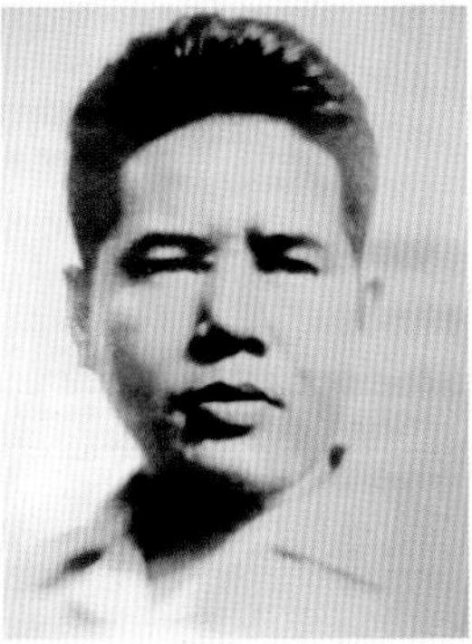

Song Ngoc Minh (Achar Mean), Chairman, Khmer Issarak movement

Assembly of monks from the districts of Kamchay Mear and Kanhchriech in Prey Veng Province chaired by Tou Samouth at Veal Ta Vong in 1953

Wearing official parliamentary dress during the Fifth Legislature of the National Assembly of the new Kingdom of Cambodia that was formed under a new constitution in 1993

Sitting in the cockpit of a Soviet MiG-21 fighter

With my wife Sao Ty (back right) and (from front left) my eldest daughter Pov, my mother, my second daughter Sam Aun, and my wife's parents after Liberation in 1979

Khmer Issarak military commanders Sok Sophay (left), So Phim (second from left), Chea Chann (middle), Neth Sinmorn (second from right) and Lim Koeurn (right) under the command of Por Kam Baou in 1953

So Phim training Eastern Zone forces at the underground base in Thlok Trach during the 1970s

With Chea Sim at the congress in Snuol District in Kratie Province on 2 December, 1978

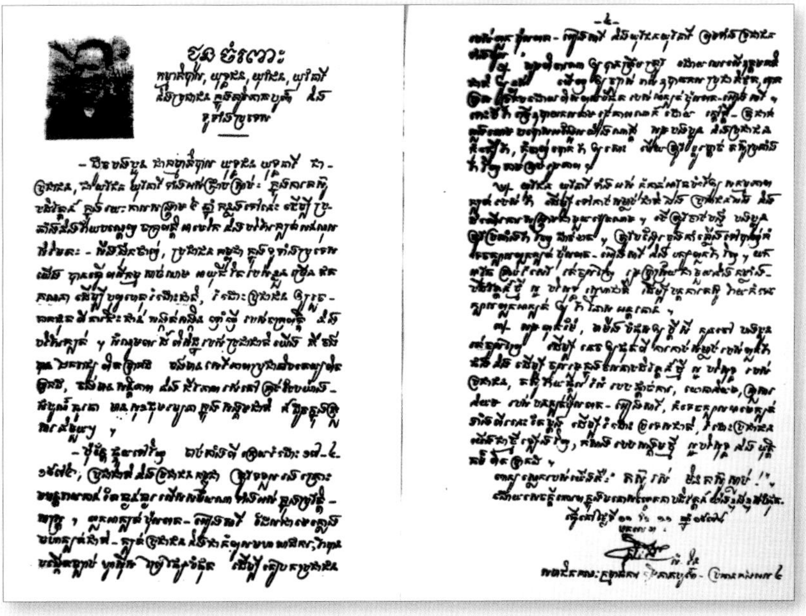

(Top) Women reading a leaflet, dated 11 November, 1978, which was dropped by air to urge all people from the Eastern Zone and across Cambodia to rise up against Pol Pot and Ieng Sary. (Above) Signed in my capacity as a member of the Eastern Zone Committee and Commander of the Fourth Division, the extract from the leaflet reads:

> *'Our motto is "struggle and survive, don't struggle and die". We clearly see all the ploys, false information and lies of the poisonous traitors…Young people, don't use your weapons to serve the activities of the traitors to kill our own people and wage the ongoing war with Vietnam. If you are forced, rise up against them…Take all weapons and ammunition into the forest and cooperate with the new revolutionary forces who are good, sincere and patriotic…Fathers, mothers, uncles and aunts, please urge your husbands, children and other relatives to flee to the forest to escape the killing and join the new revolution…to topple the extremist military regime and nepotism of Pol Pot and Ieng Sary…Destroy the heads of these two traitors, save the nation and the people to establish a new régime with genuine justice.'*

General agreement to enforce the declaration of the National Salvation Front. From left: Neou Samom, Mat Li, Bun Mi, Hem Samin, Hun Sen, Chea Sim, myself, Ros Samay, the Venerable Long Sim, Prach Sun, Chey Kanha, Mean Sam An, Chan Ven and Meas Somnang

Handing over the five-tower flag of Angkor Wat to representatives of the military

Long live the total liberation of Cambodia! Long live the People's Revolutionary Council!

(Clockwise from top left) 1-riel note, 5-riel note, 20-riel note. The new bank notes were printed in the Soviet Union and launched by the new People's Bank of Kampuchea on 20 March 1980, five years after Pol Pot's forces abolished currency.

Meeting with Comrade Le Duan (secretary general of the Communist Party of Vietnam), Comrade Pham Van Dong (prime minister), Comrade Truong Chinh (state president), in Hanoi after Liberation in 1979

Welcoming Comrade Pham Van Dong (left), the Vietnamese prime minister, to Phnom Penh on 16 February, 1979

Signing cooperation agreement with Lao People's Democratic Republic on 20 March, 1979

With Comrade Sophanouvong (left), the Lao president, visiting Phnom Penh on 6 January, 1980

With Comrade Kaysone Phomvihane (right), chairman of the Lao People's Revolutionary Party

Paying a courtesy call on Comrade Fidel Castro (right), first secretary of the Central Committee of the Communist Party of Cuba

The Joliot-Curie Gold Peace Medal
of the World Peace Council,
awarded in 1980

CAMARADE
HENG SAMRIN

Président du Conseil Populaire Revolutionnaire du Kampuchéa

République Populaire du Kampuchéa

Pour sa contribution éminente à la cause de l'indépendance national, de la Paix et de l'amitié entre les peuples.

President of the People's Revolutionary Council of Kampuchea

People's Republic of Kampuchea

For his outstanding contribution to the cause of national independence, peace and friendship between peoples.

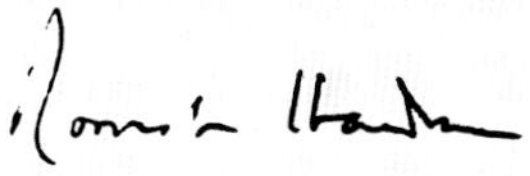

Romesh Chandra
President du Conseil Mondial de la Paix

Signing agreement with Leonid Brezhnev, general secretary of the Communist Party of the Soviet Union

Signing cooperation agreement with East German President Erich Honecker (right) in 1981

With Prime Minister Hun Sen (left) and Mikhail Gorbachev, general secretary of the Communist Party of the Soviet Union (second from right), in the 1980s

Awarding medals to Vietnamese volunteer troops and advisors who were returning home in 1988

Greeting His Majesty King Norodom Sihamoni as he arrives for a tree-planting ceremony. In 2004, King Sihamoni assumed the throne from his father, King Norodom Sihanouk, who died in 2012.

Opening session of the National Assembly, presided over by His Majesty King Norodom Sihamoni (front row, third from right) on 24 September, 2008

Chairing the 32nd meeting of the ASEAN Inter-Parliamentary Assembly (AIPA) held in Phnom Penh from 18 to 24 September, 2011

Inaugural ceremony for the 32nd meeting of the ASEAN Inter-Parliamentary Assembly (AIPA) on 20 September, 2011

Meeting with future Chinese President Xi Jinping (right) on 9 December, 2011

Meeting with Belarusian President Alexander Lukashenko (left) on 25 June, 2012

Along National Road No. 1 from Dei Edth to Veal Sbov, my forces had to swim in order to attack enemy posts. We killed some enemy soldiers and captured others. It took only a day and a night to occupy the area from Dei Edth to Veal Sbov. We confiscated arms and explosives, and gave the enemy troops a scare. They were bewildered – the battle was close to Phnom Penh and these were their last remaining posts. Although we controlled most of the battlefield, we were continually on alert and always withdrew to our camps along the Bassac River.

While stationed along the Bassac, my unit was involved in a conflict with the Southwestern Zone, which was under the command of Ta Mok. The reason for the conflict was that my unit had soldiers with malaria, and they had to stay at the main hospital in Prek Slaeng. There were shortages of medicine so I ordered my forces to look for traditional herbs in the mountains at Phnom Chiso. When they failed to return, I became anxious and dispatched three more soldiers including a company commander. All ten from the first and second dispatches disappeared. They all had documents identifying them and authorising their presence in the area. I went to ask security guards from the Southwestern Zone for an explanation. They replied that they did not know and only arrested the enemy. After that, I made a report to the Eastern Zone to seek their intervention. As commander of the zone, So Phim wrote a letter to Ta Mok. It was to be delivered personally by Oy, commander of the Twelfth Battalion. With the letter in hand, he went to see Ta Mok in Bati District in Takeo Province. He reported that when he met Ta Mok, the response was the same as when I met the security guards from his zone. Ta Mok answered that he did not know and that they arrested the enemy only. We never saw our soldiers again. Later, there was another episode along the border between Saang and Prey

Kabass districts at Prek Ambel. This was a major conflict involving infantry from the two zones exchanging mortar fire.

In late 1973, Eastern Zone Commander So Phim ordered me to withdraw my regiment from the Bassac River in Region 25 to the west of the Mekong River, redeploy to Prey Veng, and take control of the provincial hall. After arriving in the province, I let my forces camp in the village of Prey Chheu Teal in Samraong Commune, Prey Veng District. During the fighting, my forces in the 126th Regiment co-operated with the 128th Regiment led by Soeung. My regiment was assigned to the forces of the Peam Ro District Chief commanded by Sam San. The 128th Regiment was assigned to block the enemy.

In heavy fighting, my forces took the village of Doun Roeun and the Prey Veng Provincial Hall. The 128th Regiment was assigned to block the enemy from moving out of their barracks at Lok Yeay Baray, about three kilometres south of the provincial hall. We had no idea why the 128th Regiment did not carry out their duties or keep my unit informed. At dawn, enemy troops attacked my unit from behind, and many of our men were killed and wounded including Meh Mara, a deputy platoon commander. We later withdrew across a lake to the west of the provincial hall along a canal where we were attacked by 60mm and 81mm mortar. In the chaos, we crept along the canal and dropped our weapons into the water. At night, we went back to pick them all up.

Seven days after the fight for the provincial hall, the Eastern Zone ordered an attack on another enemy post at Prey Kandieng on National Road No. 1 in Peam Ro District. We destroyed the enemy post, but could not complete our mission as the 128th Regiment did not do their job in preventing enemy soldiers in the west from getting away. As a result, we killed only a small number of enemy troops.

As our superiors probably thought the 126th Regiment had the most fighting experience and battlefield success, especially after the victory at Prey Kandieng, the Eastern Zone ordered my regiment to withdraw from Prey Veng to the battlefield in Svay Rieng.

After receiving the order, we immediately moved our forces to Svay Rieng. When we arrived, I led my forces to camp in Thlok in Doun Sar Commune in Svay Chrum District. We attacked the enemy's barracks at Ou Samdei and Prey Domloung as far as National Road No. 1 to take the provincial town of Svay Rieng.

We occupied most of the area around the town so that our bases were close to the capital. The Lon Nol government officials and soldiers were worried because they could not bring in food and explosives by land. Supplies were only by plane. I remember my unit shooting down a C-130 aircraft at Troey Tahau Lake as it was on its way in to land.

Our forces had the advantage over the enemy but we could not manage to take control of the provincial capital because digging trenches during the wet season was difficult – they would collapse two or three times a day.

In December 1974, the Eastern Zone ordered my regiment to withdraw from Svay Rieng and set up positions for combat on the western side of the Mekong River and along the Bassac River (Region 25). The unit was ready for orders. After setting up the camp, we began planning to

Battlefields in Svay Rieng

attack the remaining enemy posts in cooperation with the 173rd and 160th Regiments. First we attacked Angkor Chey base, then Koki and Khsom. We took all these bases. After that, my unit continued to gather intelligence from the barracks at Ong Ko Catholic Church, Po Miev and Samraong Bridge, located south of Chrouy Dang.

Since the water level in the lake was high, it was difficult for our forces to mobilise by foot. So we attacked the enemy bases by boat. We were well prepared with provisions and set the time for the attack at 2:00 a.m. on 25 December 1974. According to plan, we started firing and pushing forward to the Samraong Bridge barracks. The other two targets were delayed till 4:00 a.m. as the thorn bushes made it difficult to advance. The attack lasted until 3:00 p.m. when we took control of the whole base. After liberation of the Ong Ko Catholic Church barracks, we moved on to Po Miev. The fighting was intense and it took 24 hours to occupy the barracks completely. We captured 300 soldiers alive, including a major.

After that, my forces went on to attack and occupy other posts such as Koki Thom, Wat Prek Thmei, Reang Dek, Kampong Phnom Krao and Kampong Phnom Knong. The enemy soldiers suffered a loss of morale, and fled across the river to the western side of Neak Loeung. My forces pushed forward to the west. On the eastern bank, enemy naval vessels were confined to Peam Ro District where the waters of the Mekong were deep. They were isolated and relied on aircraft for supplies of food and explosives. The situation was tense. Sometimes aircraft could not land, and had to use airdrops, some of which fell in our area.

The posts along National Road No. 1 and the Mekong River taken by our forces were strategically important for the Phnom Penh government, constituting one of their main supply arteries. The enemy were determined to seize them back. They immediately dispatched special forces escorted by naval vessels along the Mekong for a ground offensive to the north of Chrouy Dang Market, where our battlefield headquarters, commanded by Chan Chakrey, happened to be located. The enemy moved up on to high ground and got about 300 metres from the riverbank where they were blocked from moving forward. Since Chan Chakrey's base was under threat, I ordered my Twelfth Battalion, stationed on the western side of Neak Loeung about 15 kilometres away, to intervene. My forces had to move fast to defend the headquarters. If we were too slow, the base would be in danger and the battlefield strategy disrupted.

It was serious fighting over three days and three nights. We destroyed all the naval vessels moored along the riverbank. We also occupied all the posts west of Neak Loeung, capturing many enemy troops and confiscating a lot of arms and explosives. Many other troops ran away without looking back; some jumped into the water to swim to their vessels in the middle of the river to return to Phnom Penh.

In all these battles, thorn bushes and swamps put us at a geographical disadvantage. The enemy forces, on the other hand, were well prepared – they had dug solid trenches around each base. So the fighting was intense. Our forces nevertheless put themselves at risk in fighting for the bases; some sacrificed their lives. Our victory was complete. The soldiers we captured confessed that Lon Nol's government had no more intervention forces available, and that the régime was about to collapse. After the victory, our forces moved to gather in Kampong Phnom Krao Village. They received training in political theory, ideology and military tactics, and we were able to prepare more effectively for future engagements.

After this training, the Eastern Zone ordered my unit to plan for an attack on bases to the west of Neak Loeung in collaboration with other units of Region 20 and militia from Peam Ro, Preah Sdach and Ba Phnom in Region 24. The remaining enemy bases were on the western side of Neak Loeung, and on the eastern side where they comprised an occupied school, the Peam Ro naval base and 105mm cannons installed on the island of Koh Tachou.

Under the plan, my unit, the 126th Regiment, was assigned with other units to attack the base on the western side of Neak Loeung. The 173rd Regiment was to attack enemy forces on Koh Tachou. On schedule, all units opened fire from every direction. The enemy base was well-defended, and the fighting was fierce. My unit launched a major offensive and pushed forward, but we were hindered by the unfavourable geography.

Just as we started fighting, enemy reinforcements moved in from several directions and expanded their positions from the riverbank to the western road as far as the island of Koh Dach in Leuk Daek District. They dug several trenches for about a kilometre outside these positions and erected barbed-wire fences.

Though the enemy tried to expand and defend their remaining base, having lost their positions along National Road No.1 they were isolated. They could only move around within their base, and sustained regular artillery fire from our forces. They could bring in their supplies of food and weapons only by air. They were at a big disadvantage. Adopting a new strategy, we used our special forces to attack the enemy in their own trenches with stun grenades. Our cadres and soldiers received civilian support from the rear. We did not take long to take the western side of Neak Loeung. The remaining enemy forces lost their will to fight and were in disarray. Most jumped into the river and swam towards Koh Chamroeun island. Some had weapons; others were empty-handed.

Our battlefield commander called for an urgent meeting and made plans to attack the two enemy locations, one at Koh Chamroeun and the other at Koh Tachou. Under the plan, the commander said we needed five days to prepare our forces, but I argued for an attack on the islands that night because the defeated Lon Nol soldiers were dispirited and disorganised. So I sought approval to attack Koh Chamroeun the same night. The whole meeting agreed with my suggestion and the commander signed the order.

Chhouk Sao and I, without bodyguards, left the meeting by bicycle to return to our base about 15 kilometres north of Chrouy Dang Market. While we were riding along National Road No. 1, reaching Kampong Phnom Krao Monastery, two helicopters flying south from the Mekong River suddenly started firing at us. I dropped my bicycle and ran for shelter under a big poinciana tree by the side of the road. Chhouk Sao fell about 10 metres away. I thought he'd been hit, but when I ran over to help him up, I saw only bruises on his left hip that might have been caused by gravel. The helicopters flew away. After that, we continued our journey to the battalion headquarters to plan for the fight.

After a victory, cadres and soldiers are normally happy; any tiredness is forgotten, and the will to fight is all the stronger. Since I realised my unit felt ready to attack, I put together 20 front-line soldiers, including the commander of a regiment equipped with weapons and explosives. We set off at 10:00 p.m., reached the battlefield and opened fire at 11:30 p.m.

It was just as I had assumed – the enemy forces who had been defeated on the western side of Neak Loeung were not ready to defend themselves on Koh Chamroeun. We launched our attack, killing and injuring many of them. The survivors, who could not escape, had to jump into the Mekong River and swim to the eastern side of Neak Loeung. We took complete control of the island and none of our forces were wounded. The 173rd Regiment commanded by Chan Chakrey attacked enemy forces on the other island of Koh Tachou which, like Koh Chamroeun, was soon taken.

By that time, the remaining Lon Nol soldiers were east of Neak Loeung. The naval forces were stationed in Peam Ro. After the victory at Koh Chamroeun and Koh Tachou, I let my forces take a week off to relax and undergo political and ideological training. We needed to use our experiences as a basis for future battles.

After more than a week's rest, I received a new order from the Eastern Zone. I was to prepare my intelligence staff to gather information, and take the eastern side of Neak Loeung in collaboration with troops from Region 24 commanded by Chhouk Sao and Sin Song. To attack the enemy east of Neak Loeung at night, I assigned my unit, the 126th Regiment, to move in from the west by crossing the Mekong from Koh Chamroeun to Prek Khsay and from the north with two motorboats and three rowing boats which could each carry 10 people. Other fighters armed with light weapons would swim with the aid of floating banana tree trunks. In addition to their usual weapons, our forces would be armed with DK-82 mortars and B-40 rocket launchers.

According to plan, my forces departed at 6:30 p.m. on 29 March 1975, and travelled quietly by rowing boat to avoid being detected. If by chance we had met the enemy in the middle of the river and had had to open fire, we would have used the motorboats to head towards the east bank and move up to higher ground.

It happened as we had planned. When we got to the middle of the river, we stumbled across an enemy naval patrol moving quietly from Peam Ro to the eastern side of Neak Loeung. It was about 30 metres away. We opened fire with our B-40 rocket launchers. But we missed the target and they counter-attacked with 20mm cannons. They then quickly steered their vessel away towards Peam Ro. Seeing that, our forces quickly drove two motorboats over to rescue our men floating across the river with the banana tree trunks. They were shouting for help because they were drifting away with the current, and were not afraid of being heard by the enemy. They were finally rescued.

Given the problems involved in advancing to the enemy base at night, we delayed our attack plan until early morning. We then opened fire and surrounded their base. We attacked them to the east of Neak Loeung for two nights and three days. By 1 April 1975, we were in control of the whole area, capturing more than 1,000 government troops and confiscating both weapons and explosives.

After taking eastern Neak Loeung, the Eastern Zone ordered my unit to withdraw and leave Region 24 in charge of the area. We took only a few 81mm and 105mm shells as well as two Jeeps. We then headed back to the Bassac River where enemy forces were positioned at a swing bridge next to Boeung Thom and Koh Anlong Chen, near Kbal Koh Garrison. Under orders from the Eastern Zone, my forces launched attacks on Kbal Koh and Koh Anlong Chen and then swam along the Bassac to attack another enemy base at Prek Pra. We then began an assault on an enemy position at Champuh Kaek Monastery, the last major garrison defending Phnom Penh. We destroyed the base, seizing many tanks and weapons.

After taking Champuh Kaek Monastery, my forces crossed to the western side of the Bassac River to occupy Kandal Provincial Hall. I travelled along the national road from the hall to Chak Angre Krom with three of my bodyguards, a PC-25 field radio operator and another man called Phoeun, a battalion commander from the 173rd Regiment who also had bodyguards and a radio operator. We stopped at a cigarette factory and went inside.

Then we received a PC-25 field radio call from the enemy forces at Monivong Bridge, codenamed *romtep*. It was an offer to surrender. Using our codename *romdos*, I told them that there would be no problems if they stopped firing, put down their weapons, stored them in the garrison and came out holding white flags. After they surrendered, I went back to Kandal Provincial Hall to wait and see. It turned out that there were no explosions so they had actually followed my orders.

At 7:00 a.m. the next morning, 17 April 1975, they left the garrison and travelled along the national road from Monivong Bridge to Takhmao. Some were running and others were walking, raising white flags or holding their white shirts up. My unit headed to central Phnom Penh. As I approached the Independence Monument with the chief of the armed forces at around 9:00 a.m., some battalions went to occupy the Olympic Stadium where there were 12 abandoned helicopters.

When we arrived at the Independence Monument, we dug a trench under a banyan tree (in front of what is today the official residence of Samdech Techo Prime Minister Hun Sen). While digging the temporary trench, I saw that Lon Nol's military police had taken as their base the house of Tep Phan, mayor of Phnom Penh, surrounded by barbed wire extending from the road to the garden. Three hundred military policemen were staying there, including a major general. Some of them were so scared, they were sneaking away over the fence. I told my men to tell the major general to see me and to be their group leader, asking them not to come outside.

The military police stayed there for more than a month. To feed them, I transported rice from outside. After that, the Party Centre came and took them all from the house. They were tied to one another by the hands before being led away forever.

After my unit arrived in Phnom Penh, I was contacted by the commander of the Twelfth Division of the Special Zone. His name was Nath. His forces were located opposite enemy armoured tanks in Stueng Meanchey, which had not yet been attacked. Speaking by field radio, he called for an attack with 105mm cannons. I told him I couldn't shoot within the city because my infantry unit had already arrived there. I also told him that when I got to the Independence Monument with the military general staff, 20 representatives of the revolutionary resistance forces greeted us with flowers as the heroic national liberation army, which had just gained victory over the enemy. They were wearing black uniforms with scarves around their necks. After that, they disappeared.*

After the capture of Phnom Penh, I divided the Eastern Zone forces to take charge of the area from Monivong Bridge to Wat Phnom, and over to Monivong Boulevard in the west. We had three regiments – one led by my younger brother Heng Tal, one by me, and another by It Tat. My regiment was responsible for the area from Monivong Bridge to Wat Ounalom. After two days, we received orders from senior commanders to withdraw the other regiments, leaving mine deployed in the area from Monivong Bridge to Wat Phnom with the Cambodiana Hotel as our headquarters. Until then, I had been stationed at the house of Chuon Choeun, a senior Khmer People's Revolutionary Party member, in front of Wat Ounalom with some guards.

After the division of responsibilities for the control of Phnom

* Editor's note: *According to Ben Kiernan, founding director of the Genocide Studies Program at Yale University, the Eastern Zone forces distinguished themselves by their 'more moderate behaviour' with citizens of the capital quickly noticing the difference between the Eastern troops in khaki or green military fatigues and those entering the city from other zones. 'The ones from the west wore black, the ones from the east green. Those in black were mostly younger,' a former resident was quoted as saying.*

Penh, the Southwestern Zone warned forces from Eastern Zone not to walk across to the western side of Monivong Boulevard. Chhouk Sao, the deputy commander of my 126th Regiment, crossed the white line. He was arrested by Nath's security guards from the Twelfth Division and Special Zone Forces (who were all women). He was detained for almost a night without food until I managed to get him set free.

My unit had been guarding Phnom Penh for a month before we were replaced by a Central Forces Unit. They were all ethnic minority people from the northeast of the country. They were strict and firm – and absolute. Once they issued a command, the job had to be done without fail. After receiving the order to leave, my units withdrew our forces to the eastern side of Monivong Bridge at Chbar Ampov Market. I encamped the headquarters of the 126th Regiment at Prek Eng in Chrouy Ampil in Kien Svay District. As my forces withdrew from Phnom Penh, central security guards checked all of our backpacks before we crossed Monivong Bridge. Personal items such as toothbrushes and toothpaste were confiscated if there were more than one. But we were allowed to keep more than one hoe.

After we had taken Phnom Penh, I spent more than three months in the city before returning to the Eastern Zone. Our division held a general assembly chaired by Son Sen, chief of general staff of the Central Forces Unit, to review our strengths and weaknesses. He declared that the 173rd Regiment led by Chan Chakrey, the 126th Regiment led by me, and the 160th led by Phoeun had to be separated from the Eastern Zone to establish a Division 280 led by Chan Chakrey which would be the Party Centre's frontline division. The Party Centre decided that I would be removed from the unit and return to work in the Eastern Zone with two other people, El Kry and Heng Kim.

In July 1975, the three of us returned to the Eastern Zone. After arriving in the town of Prey Veng, we stayed at an abandoned house in the village of Doun Roeun with people from the Political Commissar Bureau. For three months, we ploughed, planted and harvested rice in a paddy field east of the town before the Eastern Zone established the Fourth Division. I was assigned to be the division commander with Reach Phorn serving as chief political commissar, Heng Kim as deputy chief for military affairs and El Kry as deputy political commissar. The division was stationed along National Road No. 7 from what is now Ponhea Kraek to Memot District in Kampong Cham Province with headquarters on a hill in Kraek. The role of the new division was to guard the national road and the Cambodian-Vietnamese border. It was also responsible for repairing the road, between Tboung Khmum District in Kampong Cham Province and Snuol District in neighbouring Kratie Province, and farming to support the livelihood of the unit.

CHAPTER 4

INTERNAL CONFLICT AND A BORDER WAR

While the Fourth Division and local people were preparing to celebrate the Party Anniversary on 30 September 1976 – with plans to hold a parade and invite many people for a feast – a telegram arrived at midnight. It was an instruction from the Party Centre, issued by Pol Pot, to postpone the celebrations nationwide and await new information. We wondered about that. We were suspicious, worried, and afraid; but nobody dared to say anything. After that, Party Centre security guards took away Chief Political Commissar Reach Phorn, who never returned. Then we saw a list of names of 'traitors', which had been sent to the Eastern Zone by the Party Centre. According to the information, those so-called traitors had made accusations against Eastern Zone Commander So Phim, regional and district chiefs and many others; but my name wasn't on the list.

Following these accusations, the Party Centre security guards 'called in' the accused one by one. The security guards told them that they would need to study or move to another place, so they were not worried. However, once called in, they never came back.

In late 1977, there was a directive to celebrate the Khmer People's

Revolutionary Party's anniversary on 30 September, putting the founding year as 1960.*

During the celebration, in a declaration to the Cambodian people and the world, the party was officially declared to be named the Communist Party of Kampuchea. Among the other key points was Pol Pot's order to the armed forces nationwide to attack Vietnam.

War broke out along the border between Cambodia and Vietnam. More than a month later, the Party Centre lost confidence in the Eastern Zone. It was suspicious and accused our zone, especially my Fourth Division, of being agents for Vietnam. It ordered my division to withdraw from the battlefield and be replaced by a division from the Northern Zone, which was commanded by Ke Pauk.

The armed forces of both countries exchanged heavy fire. As soon as the Northern Zone forces were deployed to replace my forces, the Vietnamese army launched a major offensive, attacking these forces as far as Kak Banghaeur Khlaeng in Dambae District along National Road No. 7 to the village of Pratheat, and then withdrew back into Vietnamese territory through the border checkpoints of Trapeang Phlong and Xa Mat.

The Fourth Division, under my command except for the 73rd Regiment, retreated across National Road No. 7 to Kraek Forest, located between the villages of Kraek La-ork and Ampuk. As we were moving along the road, we travelled with a Vietnamese tank division.

---

* Editor's note: *As a matter of record, the party was founded in 1951. According to historical accounts, 1960 was when Pol Pot joined the senior party leadership, ranked third behind party co-founder Tou Samouth, who disappeared in 1962, and Nuon Chea, who would become known as 'Brother No 2' after Pol Pot became secretary-general of the party in 1963. Khieu Samphan was ranked fourth. In 2014, Nuon Chea and Khieu Samphan were sentenced to life imprisonment for crimes involving the forced evacuation of people and the execution of Lon Nol's soldiers immediately after the Khmer Rouge came to power in 1975.*

We didn't open fire on them. They continued to Kak Banghauer Khlaeng as far as the villages of Korkoh and Pratheat towards Trapeang Phlong and Xa Mat checkpoints. When the Party Centre discovered the forces that had replaced us scattered in defeat, our unit was ordered to return to defend the border at Memot District, Kampong Cham Province, facing Ta Tom on the border with the Vietnamese province of Tay Ninh.

In early May 1978, So Phim issued an official letter transferring me from my position as chief of the Fourth Division to replace Keo Samnang, deputy commander of the Eastern Zone Military Headquarters in Prey Veng. After receiving the letter, I handed over my responsibilities and duties to my deputy Soeung, and promoted him commander in accordance with the decision of the zone. I left the Fourth Division headquarters in Memot on May 16 by Jeep. I was in one Jeep with my two personal bodyguards, one of whom was driving. Our bodyguard escort was in another.

When I arrived in Plark Samraong, I met Van, commander of the Seventh Division in the Northern Zone, and Ke Pauk – they were also travelling in two Jeeps. We all stopped our vehicles, shook hands and chatted – but with caution. After a while, we shook hands again and said goodbye. I soon arrived at the regional office in the town of Suong. When I met So Phim, he immediately appointed me as deputy commander and chief of general staff for the zone in Prey Veng Province.

I was in Prey Veng for only nine days when, on 25 May, a deadly power struggle broke out. The forces of Northern Zone Commander Ke Pauk, deployed in Kampong Cham near Wat Srah in Popel Commune, Ponhea Kraek District (north of where National Road No. 7 is today); while Son Sen's forces were stationed in Svay Rieng provincial headquarters along National Road No. 1.*

As a ploy to facilitate the arrest of cadres and commanders in eastern Prey Veng, Ke Pauk deceived the heads of the divisions, regiments, battalions and companies by calling an urgent meeting that included all regional Party secretaries; regional military chiefs; the two existing divisions (the Fourth and Fifth) stationed along National Road No. 7; three regiments in Regions 20, 21 and 22; and the regional office chief named Peam.

The plan was to hold the meeting at Srah Reservoir, where there was no temple at the time. When our cadres arrived at the entrance, security guards asked them – regardless of rank – to leave all weapons outside. When everyone entered a meeting room, the security guards surrounded them and pointed guns, arresting all participants. Some regional and district chiefs, who had been suspicious and did not attend the meeting, escaped into the forest to organise and launch a counter-attack.

On the same day in Svay Rieng and Prey Veng provinces, Son Sen called for a similar meeting with all commanders in the Third Division as well as the new regional commander Chan Senghong and the Eastern Zone deputy commander responsible for Regions 23 and 24. Unaware of the plot, they were all arrested and killed.

As for me, on standby in Prey Veng town, I was informed that the meetings were unusual and that none of the participants had returned. I was getting more suspicious. I assigned Khim Porn as my courier to find out what was going on along National Road No. 7 and at the regional department in Suong. When he got there, the

---

* EDITOR'S NOTE: *Son Sen was defence minister and chief of general staff of the National Army of Democratic Kampuchea. He and his family were reportedly shot to death on the orders of Pol Pot in the Khmer Rouge stronghold of Anlong Veng on the Thai border in 1997. Pol Pot himself died in Anlong Veng in 1998.*

situation was quiet. Along the road were checkpoints and people were not allowed to pass. Khim Porn tried to approach local people for additional information and fortunately met someone who advised him in a whisper not to go further: things were not good. He rushed back and reported the whole situation to me, especially the whispered warning.

I left Prey Veng that night and drove by Jeep to O'Reang Ov District in Kampong Cham with a driver and two bodyguards. It was 26 May 1978, and we slept at Wat Kong Chey near the Po-2 Hospital. At 5:00 in the morning, I went to the Tuol Preap Work Site where So Phim was staying. When I arrived, he came to meet me outside the fence of his house and I brought him back to Prey Veng Town. He agreed with my suggestion to meet with those cadres who had not attended Ke Pauk's meeting. I ordered Khim Porn to write official invitations for an urgent meeting. Among those invited were Chea Sim, the Party secretary for Ponhea Kraek District; Kong Sakun, known as Tuy, the deputy secretary for Region 20; Rin, the regional security chief; Pol Saroeun and some other district and commune cadres. The purpose of the meeting was to work out a plan to resist Ke Pauk's forces, defend the town and evacuate people – including my wife and mother – from Prey Veng Province.

At the time, I still had two naval battalions. Expecting Pol Pot's forces to start their attack, I ordered one battalion ashore to fight them around the northern end of Peam Ro Bridge and Snae Reservoir. I ordered the other along a canal as far as Kampong Trabek, near a dock southeast of the Chheu Kach Mountain, to defend the unit protecting the regional military office and sub-department staff of the Eastern Zone. This battalion would defend and patrol the area from the town of Prey Veng along National Road No. 11 to O'Reang Ov District in Kampong Cham Province. I also had two American

M-113 armoured personnel carriers to block the enemy advance on the national road.

As anticipated, Pol Pot's forces attacked us. The fighting on National Road No. 11 was intense. Since we had lost several cadres and senior commanders, who had never returned from Ke Pauk's meeting, and because the enemy had 12 Chinese tanks and helicopter support, we were pushed back to O'Reang Ov, and retreated to the village of Prey Sniet. The artillery regiment and arms division commanded by Pol Saroeun, based at the Peam Cheaang Rubber Plantation, fought the enemy at Thnal Totoeung in Chob. The fighting was fierce. We fought to clear National Road No. 7, to the north of the village of Trapeang Russei as far as Ta Pav, to join forces with Mao Phoak, commander of the weapons and ammunition warehouse in the village of Chhuk. The fighting was heavy in Trapeang Russei and Ta Pav, where there was a forest near a rubber plantation. We were surrounded and had nowhere to go, so we decided to attack and broke through the enemy forces, hiding safely in the forest of Anguoy. While sheltering there, I ordered Samneath, known as Morm, to contact the Fourth Division in Memot District for reinforcements.

After several rounds of fierce fighting, So Phim suddenly ordered a ceasefire. He assigned me to take up command as he had to go to Phnom Penh to meet Brother No. 1 to clarify the situation. He said: 'It will take only three days. If I don't return, you can keep fighting.' I urged him not to go as the situation was unusual. I thought Pol Pot planned to eliminate us all. He replied that he did not think Brother No. 1 would do such a thing. He said there would be a coup d'état by Son Sen, the national defence minister and the chief of general staff. So Phim said he had to go and find out what exactly was going on. I could read his mind – he had been a popular military leader in the Issarak movement that fought French colonial forces, and so Pol Pot trusted him and always sought his advice in war.

After telling me all this, So Phim left by Jeep and travelled through the districts of Pea Reang, Srei Santhor and Khsach Kandal, stopping at at Ak-rei Ksatr, a village across the Mekong River from Phnom Penh. He got a courier to cross the river by boat and take a letter to a bureau chief from the Party Centre, which was in Chuon Choeun's house on the eastern side of Wat Ounalom. Two hours later, the courier returned with a letter. It read: 'Please wait. Motorboats will be sent to pick you up.' An hour later, several boats arrived with security guards from the Party Centre, which was unusual.

They hit the riverbank and attacked So Phim's waiting bodyguards. Some of his guards were killed; others were arrested or fled. He was staying at the Ak-rei Ksatr Commune Hall. When he heard what had happened, he ordered the commune chief to find a horse-drawn cart to take him to Wat Kok Touch on the eastern side of Prek Champa Reservoir in Prey Sralet Commune, located in Pea Reang District in Prey Veng Province. Suffering from diarrhoea and a fever, he travelled along the Tonle Touch River towards the east of Prek Champa and stayed in Kok Touch temple with Chhean, the Party secretary for Region 22, and Sarun, logistics chief for the Eastern Zone.

I waited to hear from So Phim. Since I had received no information about him for two-and-a-half days, I felt uneasy and decided to go and look for him. I finally met him at the temple. We had a long and serious talk. He was in a state of despair. 'Don't think about me,' he said. 'Please, comrade, go back and command our forces.' However, after some discussion, So Phim agreed to come with me and stay with Yi Yon, the Party secretary in Srei Santhor District in Kampong Cham Province, whom he trusted as a long-serving former personal secretary. In Srei Santhor, we had 300 soldiers on standby for any unexpected events.

With the situation so bad, I stayed with So Phim until midnight. I then returned, but not into the town of Prey Veng. I stayed at a military brickworks in Kanhchriech District – located along National Road No. 11 in the village of Kandach Chong Ampil in Chong Ampil Commune – controlled by Chen Sao, the military leader in this region. During my stay, I assigned Nob Sovan to go into Prey Veng to tell cadres and staff from all units, including hospital personnel, to evacuate the town towards the east. Suddenly, a courier brought me a letter. It was from So Phim and written in red and black ink: 'Dear comrade, please be highly vigilant and decisive in the cause of resistance until the final drop of blood. If you are strongly determined, decisive and brave in our cause, there are only two consequences, life or death. If we die, we will die with dignity; we must not sit back and wait to be killed. I wish you success, comrade.'

After reading the letter, I couldn't sleep that night. I was worrying and thinking about it until morning. From my youth onwards, my parents were very poor and we lived in a very remote area, but I had sacrificed everything for the cause of the revolution. I was willing to fight and was victorious in various battlefields for the Party and the revolution. My only aspiration was to achieve prosperity and happiness for the Cambodian people. I had never thought of my own life. But now, for no apparent reason and after we had achieved complete victory, some of our comrades-in-arms had been smashed; soldiers who used to share the same fate in the same battlefield together were now considering each other as enemies. I found the situation heartbreaking, and felt deeply anguished.

In the morning, I called together ten officers, including Rin, the zone's security chief. I trusted Rin and assigned him to lead a team to take So Phim from Srei Santhor District to the east, close to the

Vietnamese border. Each man was equipped with an AK-47, a pack of ammunition and a B-40 rocket launcher with four rocket-propelled grenades. The commander had a handgun as well.

As they were leaving, Pol Pot's forces attacked. From Wat Svay Romiet in the distance, 12 tanks began firing shells. The division had backup from warplanes, helicopters and infantry. In fact, the enemy forces had been moving slowly overnight from O'Reang Ov District to Wat Svay Romiet, a military post in Region 20. About 6:30 a.m. the next morning, their tanks started firing shells towards the brickworks in Kandach Chong Ampil, where I was staying. They had a large number of forces moving slowly along National Road No. 11 towards the town of Prey Veng. These enemy forces were always on high alert and ready for combat. They arrived in Svay Antor District at 2:00 p.m. and stayed there overnight before moving out. It took them another three days to get to the provincial capital.

My forces didn't take any action. I let them separate into small groups and disperse quietly into the forest to wait for a chance to resume our operations. The other officers and I could not bear to face them, as we lacked so much in terms of weapons, ammunition and food. I escaped alone to the village of Prey Tbal. Later, other cadres came to the village with their families, wives and children, as well as my mother. I told them to split up and go back to their villages. With my mother and my wife, I headed for the village of Veal, located in Smaung Commune in the south of Kamchay Mear District. When we reached Veal, which was near Boeung Pou, we stayed three nights in the house of a local person. We then headed to the village of Trapeang Korkoh, where my two daughters, Pov and Samaun, had been staying with my uncle.

As I travelled with my family to Korkoh, we came across a village where some people in a collective were having a meal. We were so tired and hungry that we pleaded for some food. The leader of the collective agreed, although all that remained was rice and soup. We had no choice: we ate that and proceeded on our journey. After passing Boeung Thom Reservoir, we came across both my daughters and my uncle in Korkoh. I also met Thmenhsar, the local deputy secretary of the Party and chief of Ponhea Kraek District – he was also the adoptive father of Samneath.

I stayed there overnight with my family but did not leave with them the next morning. My mother, wife and children journeyed with Thmenhsar to the Ponhea Kraek District Office in Chhuk Sa. They then went on to Damnak Char and Chen Toung, where my mother picked up one of my sisters, and finally to my mother's village of Sambo in the commune of Kak, where I was born.

In Trapeang Korkoh, I stayed for another five days at the house of my uncle, Heng Song. I left by oxcart around 6:00 a.m. in the morning with my cousin Heng Vi, the son of Uncle Song. My cousin's wife was in front, driving the oxcart. In the back, my cousin was shielding me from the bright light of the rising sun. It was in this disguise that I travelled towards the village of Laheuy on the road between the Kanhchriech District Hall and Kamchay Mear District. I was to call on Grandpa Nhor, my cousin's father-in-law. His house was next to the national road. When we arrived, I got off the cart and greeted him. We chatted for a while before I asked him if he had a bicycle I could borrow to ride on ahead. 'I have a bicycle, but the tyre's flat,' he said. I repaired the tyre but there was no pump. After waiting for almost an hour, I borrowed a pump from someone who was cycling by. As I pumped the tyre, I looked like any ordinary man. I was wearing black shorts and a black shirt, and was covering my head with a scarf. On the back of the bicycle was a small bag.

I left Grandpa Nhor's house with my cousin and his wife. We

crossed Cheang Sin Bridge and turned left towards the villages of Tuol Sangkae and Cheach. As I was arriving at Tuol Sangkae, I came across about 300 Khmer Rouge troops. They were wearing grey clothes and heading south. I was terrified. But they did not question me – with the scarf over my face, I was able to act normally and not look at them as I cycled ahead. When I got away from them and arrived in front of Wat Cheach, I prayed to the sacred spirit of the temple to protect me.

I then rode the bicycle to the northern side of the village, and down an oxcart path past a rice field that led to a forest. At the village of Damnak Tae, I had to lift the bicycle as I crossed the Tames Reservoir – the water came up to my chest. As I made my way to the village of Dang Kdaong, I got lost. I asked the local villagers to show me the way. They were very friendly and asked where I'd come from. 'I've come from Cheach Village, across the Tames Reservoir,' I said. They were worried for me – security forces from Region 20 had been in the area and had left only the day before. I froze for a moment. Then I said goodbye, heading off to find Dang Kdaong.*

Next to one village, I came across a paddy field with a big wild almond tree (*derm chambok*). I saw children playing under the shade of the tree and hid my bicycle in bushes well away from the road. I approached the children normally and asked the name of the village. 'Sambo,' they replied. I then asked where the people came from. 'Anlong Chrey and Thlok Trach.' I asked one boy the name of his parents. 'I'm a grandson of Grandpa Huon,' he said. I was so happy – Huon was my older brother's name. I went back to retrieve my bicycle and found my older brother as well as my wife and children.

After that, I lived with them as a farmer, transplanting and

---

* EDITOR'S NOTE: *Region 20 was in eastern Prey Veng Province close to the border with Vietnam.*

harvesting rice. But I could enter the village only at night. During the day, I hid along a canal. The village Khmer Rouge spies often walked back and forth around my family's house. They often asked Sao You, my father-in-law, if he'd seen any high-ranking people. 'I've never seen any high-ranking people,' he used to say. My father-in-law told me about that at night. I was worried, and thought about the future. It would not be peaceful. At the end of May 1978, I decided to leave the village, abandoning my children and the rest of my family. I would greatly miss them.

CHAPTER 5

THE FIGHT AGAINST POL POT

I always remembered So Phim's advice. There are only two ways: 'life or death'. If we were going to die, we would do so with dignity. We couldn't submit, and wait to be killed. So Phim never made it to Vietnam. Yi Yon, the secretary of Srei Santhor District, who was also his former personal assistant, fled north toward Region 21 amid growing unrest in the Eastern Zone. Enemy aircraft distributed leaflets accusing Eastern Zone Commander So Phim of being a traitor; the deputy secretary of the district, a man called Han, ordered troops to kill him. In armed clashes between his bodyguards and the district troops, So Phim was killed in Prek Pou, the then district capital. Also killed were his wife Phan, also known as Grandma Karo, and two of their children. They used his body as evidence that the accusations of treachery against him were true and that he was in fact dead. Chhean, the party secretary for Region 22, and Sarun, the logistics chief for the Eastern Zone, were also killed.*

I had no choice. I decided to leave my family and go back to the forest to keep fighting. For human beings, the love for families is truly deep – it cannot be measured. When I left them, they were

---

* EDITOR'S NOTE: *Region 22 was in western Prey Veng Province.*

weeping. They thought that I would never return. I felt nostalgic for the past, and wondered what their future would be. How would things turn out? As I was leaving, I had no idea where to go.

As I walked, I thought deeply about my own future. When I reached Tatork Forest, south of Doun Nhorng, I hid there for five days. I saw Pol Pot's forces evacuating all the villagers. They shot dead a man called Sok Min as a warning to others who might resist. Then they assembled the terrified inhabitants and ordered them to leave without their belongings, except for the clothes they were wearing. Cattle, houses and other property were abandoned. The villagers were separated. Some were ordered to live in the villages of Bos, Dauntei and Kandaol Chrum. Others were forced to live as far away as O'Reang Ov.

During the evacuation, Pol Pot's forces questioned villagers one by one, in search of a lady called Rai, the former head of the Women's Association in Ponhea Kraek District who was travelling with them. The villagers were terrified. When they arrived at Kanhchae Village, Rai escaped through a paddy field to the west. Pol Pot's forces saw her and opened fire with AK-47s. Fortunately, they missed her as she tripped over an embankment and fell. When they saw her falling, they shouted that they had hit their target and stopped shooting. She stood up and ran as fast as she could into the forest nearby. She survives today and, although quite elderly, still lives in Phnom Penh with her children.

After the failed attempt to kill Rai, all the men who had been evacuated escaped to the east of the forest. Finding the situation changed, Pol Pot's forces fired M-79 grenade launchers into the forest, determined to keep killing people from the village. My sister-in-law, who happened to be in the area, was slightly wounded in the hip.

As events became more complicated, I gathered together the

villagers who had escaped into the forest to form a resistance movement. I was the leader, Chea Sim was my deputy and some other members included my brother Heng Samkai, Sim Ka and Hem Bo. Later, this movement persuaded a battalion led by Seang Hay, deputy commander of the 280th Division, to rebel against the Krabao military camp in Kamchay Mear District in Prey Veng Province. We seized firearms, ammunition, and other equipment including a vehicle, which we hid in the forest.

However, we faced many difficulties – we did not have a support base and we were short of weapons, ammunition, food and medicine. We had tried to contact the Vietnamese side to help the hundreds of thousands of people who had fled into the forest, but faced many obstacles, since the Khmer Rouge had laid so many landmines along the Cambodian-Vietnamese border and strictly patrolled the area.

I tried to get assistance from Vietnam by any means possible. Many of our men were killed or injured while trying to make contact, but we eventually got through. To open a border crossing, we co-operated with Vietnamese military volunteers, some of whom lost their lives. At this point, I was based south of National Road No. 7, near Prey Tatork, with others including Chea Sim, Sim Ka and Heng Samkai. The rest had scattered into small groups, and were not familiar with the situation. There were misconceptions and no common goal. I was worried. I assigned a messenger to contact these groups but without success – when he came back, the messenger said he either couldn't find them or had no information at all. After agreeing with Chea Sim and Sim Ka to look for the cadres and soldiers who were in hiding, I happened to meet So Phaeng (now known as Phorn Phaeng). Then I learned that the men – including Mao Phoak, Ouk Bun Chhoeurn, Sa Bun, Chan Seng, Mat Ly, Say Chhum, Pol Saroeun, So Nal, Tith Ream and others – were north of National Road No. 7.

After receiving this information, I headed north with So Phaeng, Heng Samkai and Yoak Cheak to find them, crossing from Sbek Kue, Bot Tonlear, Trapeang Chhlus and into a teak forest, and then from Andongluk through Chhorkneak Creek into Anguoy Forest. We first met forces of Region 21 led by Ouk Bun Chhoeurn, Sa Bun, Chan Seng, Tith Ream, Khoun Ran and others.

So they could understand the situation, I had a meeting and informed them that Pol Pot and his men were carrying out a purge of the Eastern Zone. I told them clearly that the Party Centre led by Pol Pot was taking measures to kill leaders at all levels in our zone. The betrayal had been planned for ages but had become obvious when Pol Pot issued orders to cancel the Party's 25th anniversary on 30 September 1976, when the Party and people in the east had prepared for a big celebration.

Many cadres and people wondered about that but nobody dared to speak out. Then in 1977, the Party Centre had ordered celebrations for the founding of the Party in 1960 instead of 1951. It was a betrayal by the Party Centre led by Pol Pot. I proposed that Ouk Bun Chheourn, deputy secretary of the Party in Region 21, find a way to communicate with Vietnam, at the border checkpoint in Memot District, to get help so we could fight back, because we faced many obstacles and were being relentlessly pursued.

I stressed that there were plans to dissolve the top leadership of the Eastern Zone and that they did not clearly understand the situation. After I finished briefing them, I got negative reactions from Ouk Bun Chheourn, Mao Phoak and Khuon Ran. 'Brother No. 1 is not like that,' they said, referring to Pol Pot. Sa Bun agreed with me but Chan Seng was reluctant.

Without an agreement, four of us travelled to a military camp about five kilometres from the Region 21 Headquarters. The camp had five battalions under the direct command of Mao Phoak and Pol Saroeun. They were also members of the military committee for the Eastern Zone, which was under my direct control as deputy commander of the zone. After staying there for a day, I called a meeting with 30 members of the battalion's general staff including Say Chhum, Pol Saroeun, So Nal, Phan, Choy and Msas Loh. I repeated what I had said at the earlier meeting with Region 21. I briefed them about the situation and the actions that the Pol Pot Party Centre had taken against the Eastern Zone. After my briefing, they accepted what I had said, and expressed their belief in our forces continuing to fight. As I shared my remaining tobacco and smoked with them, we seemed to forget about our worries for a while.

I remembered that on this happy occasion, one man with tobacco but no paper ran to get rolling paper from his bag. He found only a small notebook, 'Special Youth Flag', which had been recently confiscated from an enemy camp near Chhuk Village in Krouch Chhmar District, Kampong Cham Province. The notebook was issued in early June, 1978. When I was about to tear a piece of paper to roll a cigarette, I found a list of people who had been accused by Pol Pot of being traitors to the revolution in 1969 and 1970, such as Chan Samorn, also known as Grandpa Min, and Nam San.

Seeing the list of people who had been killed by Pol Pot, I said the book was an important piece of evidence. As he was handing it to me, the man holding the book said my briefing seemed to be consistent with what we saw in the book. I later developed propaganda based on this book, so our military forces and other people could more clearly appreciate the betrayal by Pol Pot, and no longer have any doubts.

Understanding the benefits of such propaganda, we prepared tens of thousands of leaflets to condemn Pol Pot's treacherous policy, and distributed them to all our bases as an inspiration to stand up against Pol Pot's forces.

I later assigned 50 soldiers, armed with rifles, a DK-75 weapon and a DK-82 mortar, to Say Chhum and Heng Samkai, my older brother. They crossed to the south of National Road No. 7 to join forces with Chea Sim. I stayed at the camp to communicate with the Fourth Division under the command of Samneath.

Around this time, a disastrous event took place. Mao Phoak ordered the arrest and execution of Phan, a member of the general staff, for immoral relations with a lady. As soon as I heard about this, I ordered Mao Phoak to release the man and send him back to his unit. Mao Phoak later ordered the arrest and execution of Sa Kun, a senior officer who specialised in 105mm artillery. I had no idea why he did this and intervened, this time warning Mao Phoak, and instructing him never to order these types of executions again as the soldiers needed to survive – that was why they had fled to the forest for the resistance.

Since Mao Phoak kept having such internal conflicts with the team, we suspected he was a spy. Despite my warnings, he later ordered the arrest of Sar Kheng, who fled the camp to stay with Chea Sim in Prey Tatork, south of National Road No. 7. After this failed attempt to arrest Sar Kheng, Mao Phoak continued to execute our men, accusing them of immorality or betrayal. We got the impression that he was careless in carrying out his duties. After fighting the enemy, he used to gather local people in the forest. There were probably agents among them since the enemy knew where we were hiding – Pol Pot's forces later attacked local residents and our units in the village of Baray and at Krobei Kreak Base, where almost everything was destroyed.

Before these attacks, because of our suspicions about Mao Phoak I had led a force of more than one hundred soldiers out of the base, accompanied by Pol Saroeun, Yi Yon and other high-ranking officers. We were armed with rifles, 12mm machine guns and 60mm mortars as well as DK-75 and DK-82 weapons. We were lucky – our two units came under attack when we were about 10 kilometres from our base.

Our forces at the two bases did not counterattack on a large scale. Instead, we tried to defend ourselves and then withdrew. We split up into small groups, with plans to regroup in the Laokroporn area in Memot District in an attempt to contact Vietnamese troops stationed along the border. Since the Memot border was a strategic location, another group made contact with the Vietnamese before us. To negotiate with their Vietnamese counterparts, they delegated Mao Phoak, Ouk Bun Chhoeurn, So Nal and Khoun Ran and others. They raised some issues to be negotiated, but the two sides did not reach a conclusion.

My forces and several hundred villagers decided to head for Kampong Meanchey, which was more convenient for us. We travelled through the southern part of Prek Anlongrun toward Kampong Meanchey. When we approached an unpaved road, I ordered my men and another regiment to walk south, deploying forces to patrol on the lookout for enemy troops. Once the area was believed to be secure, my messenger led us to the road. But when we were about to cross the road, we suddenly encountered enemy fire and were forced to retreat to our previous position. Some of our forces ended up on the south of the road and clashed with Pol Pot's forces the following morning. Fortunately, nobody on our side was injured and they crossed back to the northern side of the road. The enemy continued to patrol the road. They did not dare enter the forest, but they were constantly firing with M-79 grenade launchers.

The situation was extremely tense and came to a standstill. With the enemy focusing on the southern and eastern parts of the

Cambodian-Vietnamese border and ignoring the northern stretch of National Road No. 7, we headed north after three days of attacks. As there were torrential rains and floods, we moved with difficulty towards Chhorkneak Creek into Anguoy Forest, passing by Pratheat, Dambae and Chhlong next to Kampong Raing Bridge to the east. We then passed the villages of Kporb, Laokroporn, Chhuer Khlem and Ponley before reaching Koki Village in Memot District. When we arrived at Koki, we found a cornfield where we picked some corn and winter melons. My men were about to shoot a musk deer running in front of us but I stopped them.

About 15 minutes after leaving the cornfield, we suddenly heard a shot. 'Who's firing?' I asked. The men in front said it wasn't our forces so I ordered everyone back into the forest assuming there'd be a problem. When we went into the forest, we saw many Vietnamese trenches and after a while our intelligence officers reported that the fire was coming not from the enemy but from Vietnamese soldiers. I ordered my men to move out of the forest. As we were about to leave, Pol Pot's forces opened fire on our forces with several B-69 grenade launchers. I immediately ordered my men to lie down and listen carefully to establish where the shooting was coming from. Heng Samkai and I lay down with eight bodyguards, waiting to see what would happen.

After the firing stopped, we stood up and called for the other men but there was no response. As we looked for them, I went about 100 metres off the path and found them heading towards the village of Cham Kchong. We'd been walking for three days and three nights. We drank only water and had no meals since the cooking pot and food were with the group at the front. As we were about to cross a road leading to Koki about 5:00 p.m., we saw villagers walking with their children and belongings. They were probably heading towards the villages of Cham Kchong and Memong in Memong Commune in Memot District. We were on high alert and waited for the villagers to pass before crossing the road. As we did, the enemy opened fire from a distance. Faced with several B-69 grenade launchers, the villagers panicked and ran into the forest to the south of the road where we were, although most of them missed us.

As we observed the situation, a young woman around 20 years old suddenly appeared with two children, one holding her hand and the other hugged to her chest. When we met her, she asked to go with us. Since it was getting dark and we didn't know where to go, we decided to find a place to rest, allowing the woman to sleep in the middle of our group with her two kids. By about 9:00 p.m. they were sound asleep, so we quietly crawled away and crossed the road to the east to sleep near the village of Cham Kchong.

At dawn, we heard multiple gunfire between Vietnamese troops and Pol Pot's forces, possibly in Memot. We were still at Cham Kchong. We heard the noise of people digging, about 100 metres south of our position. And then we heard a 105mm shell falling not too far behind us. We had no idea where it was coming from. The sound of digging was coming from Pol Pot's forces. They were digging trenches. Perhaps the Vietnamese troops knew the local geography. In any case, they started to attack Pol Pot's infantry who soon fled, leaving two soldiers dead on the battlefield, close to our position. We could see the Vietnamese troops clearly so we introduced ourselves to them.

The Vietnamese disarmed us, taking 10 weapons including two K-54 pistols that belonged to Heng Samkai and myself. They took everything from us except our clothes. However, they treated us well. They cooked rice and offered us food to eat, and then started questioning my brother and me as they suspected there must be two senior Khmer Rouge leaders in our group. In my first interrogation, I hid my identity, telling them my name was Mien. I don't know whether they were seeking more information or were still suspicious, but at 7:00 p.m. the Vietnamese commander sent us to Memot.

In every country, soldiers who surrender in battlefields are considered prisoners of war who should be treated accordingly. In our case, the Vietnamese soldiers showed respect and apologised to me before they tied our hands together. I asked whether we could be untied. 'Not allowed,' we were told. 'This is the military rule.' My bodyguards were shocked at seeing me tied up and afraid I'd be executed Pol Pot-style. I told them about the rules of war and urged them to calm down. Unlike Pol Pot's forces, the Vietnamese were not trying to kill us. 'We've come here to survive and now we've reached a safe place,' I said. 'If they take us away to be killed, we'll die without any regrets.' The Vietnamese troops did not handcuff us but tied our wrists with hammock nylon. I was first in line followed by Heng Samkai and the rest. When we arrived in Memot, we were allowed to stay at a Vietnamese military camp in the village of Sangkum Meanchey where they cooked for us again. After the meal, they conducted a second interrogation of both Heng Samkai and myself. They then allowed us to sleep all together under a tent, which had been set up on the ground floor of a cottage. I asked if I could put up a hammock but it wasn't allowed.

A third interrogation started at 7:30 a.m. the next morning. As we were about to start a fourth at 9:30 a.m., by either luck or destiny they changed to a new interpreter. 'That's Samrin!' he shouted from about 30 metres away. He knew me and I could not deny it. He approached and hugged me. 'Samrin! Samrin!' The Vietnamese troops surrounded us and cheered. They had been told to look for Muoi Su, an alias for So Phim, and another individual by the name of Samrin who had been living with him for many years. After this, the Vietnamese troops freed us and provided accommodation for us to live with them and have three meals a day. Our confiscated weapons were all returned.

We lived with our Vietnamese comrades for almost two weeks before we were sent to a big unit based at a rubber factory in Khnong Kroper, where Mao Phoak and Ouk Bun Chhoeurn called for a meeting of all cadres including me. At the start of the meeting, Ouk Bun Chhoeurn raised two items on the agenda. The first was identifying the Cambodian team to negotiate with Vietnam. The second was re-establishing the headquarters of the Eastern Zone and choosing a new leader. Ouk Bun Chhoeurn said he was the leader of the negotiating team followed by Mao Phoak, Khoun Ran and So Nal as members among others.

Ouk Bun Chhoeurn raised some problems with the Vietnamese but no agreement was reached. He later raised the issue of re-establishing the Eastern Zone and choosing a new commander. He first chose me as the new commander but I argued that it was not yet necessary. We did not have enough suitable bases and did not clearly understand the situation, so we could only nominate a small team. I was already the leader of the resistance movement with Chea Sim as my deputy. During that meeting, Mao Phoak and Ouk Bun Chhoeurn disagreed with me, both persisting with the argument for re-establishing the zone and appointing a new commander. Ouk Bun Chhoeurn then appointed himself as commander with Mao Phoak as his deputy in charge of military affairs. The meeting was adjourned.

In due course, our accommodation was divided. I had to stay at Tromeng near the border and the other soldiers stayed at the rubber factory. We were there for eight days before the Vietnamese commander called Ouk Bun Chhoeurn for an urgent meeting with some others at the factory. Ouk Bun Chhoeurn passed by the place where I was staying, let me know that the Vietnamese side had asked him to attend the meeting, and asked me whether I wanted to go with him or not. I agreed to accompany him. When we arrived at the rubber factory, we met a Vietnamese colonel by the name of Ba Ha who had invited Ouk Bun Chhoeurn and Mao Phoak also to attend. Ba Ha could not speak Khmer but through his interpreter said: 'It's you, Samrin!' He told me that he had been searching for me but had not been able to find me – Cambodian soldiers had lied to him, saying that I was not there. 'But now I see you.' He asked me to accompany him to meet his superiors, who had been looking for me. I agreed but asked whether we could meet the next day as it was already 4:00 p.m. 'That's okay,' he said. 'Can I come with three other men?' I asked. He agreed. The men I would take were Pol Saroeun, Yi Yon and Hem Bo. Since I was accompanying the colonel to Vietnam the next day, I told Ouk Bun Chhoeurn that I could not attend the meeting with him as I had to get back to where I was staying.

I left the next morning with nothing but my patched clothes covered in mud and dust. Say Chhum, my personal secretary, kept my possessions – a K-54 pistol, an American military bag with a radio, a set of new black clothes, a nylon hammock and some other stuff. It was 7:00 a.m. when we reached the agreed location, and boarded an aircraft in the company of several other people. I will never forget my first experience of flying. We were so excited. None of us ever imagined we would get to fly. We had been living in forests and mud, away from our wives and children – horrible lives in which we sometimes faced death. We could never have imagined flying with such great honour and fame. About two hours after taking off, we landed at Tan Son Nhat Airport in Ho Chi Minh City. We saw many people in nice clothes waiting to welcome us. After the engines had stopped, we disembarked and were offered flowers. Greeting us on arrival were Chea Sim, Sim Ka, Ros Chhun, Heng Samkai and some others. Overwhelmed, I rushed to hug them and could barely contain my tears. Having been separated in the chaos of conflict, while our enemies were trying to kill us, we never expected to see each other again.

It was an international reception, magnificently organised. After greeting Chea Sim, Sim Ka and the others, I was invited to get into a beautiful small car and driven away to a guesthouse. When we arrived, the car stopped in front of the stairs, which had a red carpet. I had never been offered such a great reception. Inside the guesthouse were tailors waiting to take measurements and cut clothes for me. After getting measured, I was invited to go up to rest in a room that had been reserved for me. It had a red carpet with a bed, a wardrobe with a mirror and a nice picture hanging on the wall. I took a short rest and then went out for lunch. My newly cut clothes were brought to me afterwards. As I got dressed, my old clothes were taken away to be washed. They were ironed and nicely folded before being handed back to me.

After that, I had meetings with Vietnamese leaders. The first was with Le Duc Anh, the major general in charge of the Southern Military Region based in Ho Chi Minh City; he was also a member of the Politburo of the Communist Party of Vietnam. Later, I held talks with Politburo member Le Duc Tho, Secretary-General of the Central Committee and head of the Central Organising Committee of the Communist Party of Vietnam. In welcoming me, they expressed their love, respect and friendliness to me and the people of Cambodia as brothers. We discussed the suffering of Cambodia: the country was being being destroyed and the people killed by Pol Pot – which they already knew.

I proposed that Vietnam should assist Cambodia – which, under the régime of Pol Pot, Ieng Sary, Khieu Samphan and Son Sen, was experiencing disaster – and save the hundreds of thousands of Cambodians who were living in the forest and facing difficulties. These included being hunted down and brutally killed by Pol Pot's troops along the Cambodian-Vietnamese border.

All these requests were well-received by the Vietnamese leaders, who expressed their support; they started processing my proposals to help develop principles and draft a policy for the establishment of a United Front for the National Salvation of Kampuchea.

In due course, draft statutes with 11 policies for the Front were developed for discussion. Eight of us took part in the discussions (myself, Chea Sim, Hun Sen, Pen Sovann, Ros Samay, Bou Thong, Bun Mi and Soeuy Keo) along with some notetakers. After the 11 points were developed, we organised – with the support of Vietnam – an historic general assembly on Vietnamese territory on 28 November 1978. Its task was to adopt these policies and nominate the 14 leaders of the Front. I was chairman, Chea Sim was deputy chairman and Ros Samay was secretary-general. The other members of the Front were Hun Sen, Mat Ly, Bun Mi, Mean Sam An, Meas Somnang, Neou Samom, the Venerable Long Sim, Hem Samin, Chey Kanha, Chan Ven and Prach Sun.

After that meeting, we organised a big congress in the village of Choeung Klou in Choeung Klou Commune in Snuol District in Kratie Province on 2 December to announce that Cambodia had a National Salvation Front and present its leaders to the country and the world. At the congress, I announced the 11-point policy. I declared that the Front had been established 'in the spirit of independence and virtues of the Cambodian people to unite all citizens across the country and to bring together – irrespective of politics and religion – all patriots including workers, farmers, intellectuals, the middle class, monks, current ruling power patriots and emigrants living abroad regardless of age or gender to be reunited in both spirit and ideas to overthrow the nepotistic reactionaries Pol Pot and Ieng Sary, who were extreme militarists and puppets of foreign reactionary forces.' It was formed also to 'erase the brutality and bloodshed of their régime to build a new democratic people's republic to develop the Angkor traditions, to make Cambodia a truly peaceful, independent, democratic, neutral and non-aligned country advancing to socialism, thus contributing actively to the common struggle for peace and stability in Southeast Asia'.*

To these ends, the principal undertakings of the National Salvation Front were to:

(1) unite all forces nationwide to topple the militaristic, radical régime of Pol Pot, Ieng Sary, and to dissolve the National Assembly set up by Pol Pot and Ieng Sary; and to: organise elections nationwide to elect members of the National Assembly, establishing the authority of a democratic republic at all levels; and establish a new constitution to guarantee freedom, rights, equality and democracy for our people and develop laws for the country with independence and democracy advancing to socialism;

(2) set up large revolutionary citizens' associations for youth, women, farmers and intellectuals as members of the National Salvation Front to educate people and gather them from various places to destroy the reactionary Pol Pot-Ieng Sary clique and dissolve collectives to make Cambodians the owners of the country;

(3) build and expand revolutionary forces with the Cambodian people to destroy the authority of the Pol Pot-Ieng Sary clique and protect revolutionary power as well as people's lives and property to increase the defence of our motherland

---

* *EDITOR'S NOTE: Angkor, located in present-day Siem Reap, was the centre of the Khmer Empire from the 9th to the 15th centuries. The Khmer Empire encompassed much of Southeast Asia. Angkor played a formative role in the political and cultural development of the region.*

with independence, sovereignty, national ownership rights and people's values;

(4) fully implement democracy and freedom of rights, respecting human rights and values. All Cambodians have the right to return to their homelands and rebuild their family lives in happiness. All Cambodians have freedom of residence and movement, the right to stand for election and vote, freedom of thought, association and religion, and the right to work, recreation and education. The physical rights of the people are to be ensured. To live in our society in Cambodia, everyone has equal access to rights and freedoms and they share common obligations and benefits;

(5) carry out independent economic principles towards socialism, reconstruct the war-torn country and rebuild the economy destroyed by Pol Pot and Ieng Sary. The new economic sphere is an economy to serve the common benefits of the people based on strengthening and expanding agriculture and industry with a well-planned economy appropriate to market demands towards socialism which will: eliminate the forced system of collective work and meals; eliminate the confiscation of people's rice and property by the Pol Pot-Ieng Sary clique; support and encourage all aspects of mutual assistance on the basis of voluntary cooperation among newly-conscious farmers to promote better production and livelihoods of the people; set up banks to promote the use of currency and expand the exchange of goods; broadly open local businesses and increase economic cooperation with other countries, based on equality as well as common and mutual benefits; eliminate the culture of forcing people to overwork that Pol Pot and Ieng Sary enforced in their régime; and implement an eight-hour working day and provide allowances in accordance with the principles of benefits based on work performance;

(6) replace forced marriages with free marriages and: rebuild the livelihoods and happiness of each family, enforce equal rights between men and women and provide favourable conditions for education, culture and vocational training for women to serve society equally to men; pay attention and provide support to the handicapped and the families of veterans who either died during wartime or paid tribute to the revolution; pay attention to people's welfare, supporting elderly and handicapped people as well as vulnerable orphans; and protect the interests of Cambodian emigrants living abroad and have proper regulations for immigrants living in Cambodia;

(7) eliminate the culture of the reactionary Pol Pot-Ieng Sary clique to rebuild a patriotic culture; abolish illiteracy; expand public education by establishing schools teaching the national language from primary to higher education and

vocational training; pay more attention and create jobs for skilled labour in science, technology, culture and the arts; maintain, promote and reconstruct national heritage, temples and gardens, which were destroyed by Pol Pot and Ieng Sary;

(8) welcome and provide favourable conditions for soldiers – and cadres and staff belonging to the treacherous authorities – who joined us, to fight against Pol Pot and Ieng Sary to rescue the nation and motherland; strongly condemn the uncompromising traitors for perpetrating crimes against the people; pardon those who are honest and acknowledge their wrongdoings; admire and appreciate reasonably those who were devoted to the revolution; and treat well the soldiers and civil servants of Pol Pot and Ieng Sary captured in battle and help them become good citizens;

(9) adhere to principles of international peace, friendship and non-aligned status irrespective of political systems based on peaceful co-existence and mutual respect for sovereignty, independence, territorial integrity, non-interference in each other's internal affairs, equality and common interest;

(10) peacefully resolve controversial issues with neighbouring countries based on mutual respect of independence, sovereignty and territorial integrity; end the war along the Vietnamese border caused by Pol Pot and Ieng Sary; and restore bonds of ties, friendship and good cooperation with neighbouring countries as well as other countries in Southeast Asia to build a centre of peace, independence, freedom, neutrality, stability and prosperity in the region. Cambodia shall never get involved with any military alliance and never allow any country to instal military bases or bring any kind of weaponry into the country;

(11) strengthen solidarity with all revolutionary forces and progressive countries around the world; commit to support the cause of people's resistance in other countries for peace, independence, democracy and social progress; and oppose both new and old colonial forms of imperialism.

The declaration of the National Salvation Front's political platform was a historic event, and clearly showed our determination to liberate and rebuild our nation. The atmosphere among the assembly participants was joyful, excited, and also nostalgic as they saw the Front's new flag with the five-tower temple in the centre, symbolising Cambodian civilisation and the blood shed by our cadres, government officials and people for the cause of independence and freedom. I officially handed the flag over to Keang Savuth, representative of the entire military, to free the nation as soon as possible. The founding members of the Front, representing every part of the revolutionary movement which I led, declared to the congress that we were committed to transform the declaration into action to achieve victory over Pol Pot and rebuild our country.

After the meeting, the declaration was made public. It appealed to all Cambodians – regardless of race, religion, political affiliation or occupation – to unite under the single flag of the Front; and to stand together, topple the régime and save our motherland from the iron grip of Pol Pot. The declaration appealed to all people, countries and international organisations striving for peace, independence, democracy and social progress across the world to support the struggle of the Cambodian people.

The people of Cambodia were used to living under repression, but under Pol Pot they were being even more harshly repressed: so when they heard about the declaration they were determined to fight the régime — everyone in the liberated or affected zones was enthusiastic and excited. In the liberated areas, led by various committees, people gathered for big meetings to support the declaration. They agreed to send their children, husbands and grandchildren to join the movement and expressed their commitment to increase rice production in support of the Front.

As news of the declaration spread, the United Front mushroomed. As a result of efforts by its leaders and support from friendly countries around the world, especially Vietnam, a radio station named Voice of the Kampuchean People was set up on 3 December 1978. Initially the station had only 33 staff, but it did its utmost to broadcast the principles of the Front and other information which contributed to the movement's achievements. At the same time, a news agency called Sar Pormean Kampuchea (SPK) was established.

The launch of the radio station and SPK not only contributed to the progress of the movement but also offered an opportunity for countries across the world and the Cambodian people to follow the movement, which was getting stronger. Given the clear principles of the Front, people were ready to support it.

In areas freed from Pol Pot's control, National Salvation associations were established – for women, youth, intellectuals and trade unions – to help reinforce the movement's collective power. These associations facilitated the widespread distribution of propaganda, capturing people's attention and inspiring feelings of revenge, a desire to fight. The build-up of military forces was meanwhile gaining pace, culminating in the formation of about 30 battalions. It was not long before our forces joined with Vietnamese volunteer troops in launching attacks against the enemy in Mondulkiri, Kratie, Kampong Cham and Svay Rieng; 335 enemy soldiers were killed and 70 arrested. We confiscated considerable amounts of weapons and food.

One by one, areas were liberated and people's committees and mass revolutionary organisations set up at all levels. Every organisational structure established by Pol Pot was destroyed. In these areas, freedoms and rights were restored – such as travelling, talking, eating, returning to former homes, religion, marriage, labour and holidays – and a new economic sphere was born. Despite complications and challenges, authorities in areas controlled by the Front paid close attention to making it possible for children to go to school. Everything destroyed by the Pol Pot régime was being restored and developed. The people were delighted, and gave us their support.

Under the leadership of the Front, our forces launched major attacks against the enemy, especially in the east and northeast, and in some other zones where the Pol Pot régime had been destabilised. In some zones, Pol Pot's forces lost control. People in Chhlong District in Kratie Province and Krouch Chhmar District in Kampong Cham Province, for example, had already agreed overwhelmingly to demand democratic freedoms, happiness, and the end of things such as overwork and military conscription. They were condemning leaders who acted harshly, and demanding an end to Pol Pot's rule. The administration of the régime was being seriously challenged over life-and-death issues, its inhumanity, and it was unable to solve problems.

The launch of the Front showed how far the movement had progressed from day to day. The military forces of the Pol Pot régime had been expanded from about seven divisions in 1975 to 23 divisions in 1978, all well equipped with weapons; it was nevertheless being shaken by our attacks, supported by the Vietnamese.

In the uprising, the Cambodian movement was joined by the party, government, army, and people of Vietnam. All these elements shared a common goal, to topple the Pol Pot régime. After receiving requests for assistance from the United Front's leaders, Vietnam transformed a border war against Pol Pot into a full-scale war, providing extensive support to the Cambodian movement in its efforts to overthrow the Pol Pot régime. The special units sent by Pol Pot to invade Vietnam were defeated and destroyed by the people and army of Vietnam.

The headquarters of our Revolutionary Armed Forces and National Salvation Front decided to instigate an uprising against Pol Pot. The assaults against the régime's forces were widespread.

Before the Northern Zone was liberated by the United Front and

Vietnamese forces, the Pol Pot forces deployed two divisions in their defence. The 108th Division had been based in Ou Ya Dav District in Ratanakkiri Province, while the 920th Division was stationed in Mondulkiri Province. These two divisions had built up exceptional expertise and had gained full battlefield experience in the war against the US and its allies. Pol Pot was confident.

United Front forces in this area were the 578th Battalion with more than 500 soldiers, mostly from ethnic minorities and supported by the Fifth Military Region of the People's Army of Vietnam. The battalion was in charge of liberating the provinces of Ratanakkiri, Mondulkiri, Stung Treng and Preah Vihear – all the way to temples on the peak of the Dangrek Mountains. Our units in this region were carrying a heavy responsibility – the area stretched from the Vietnamese border across the highlands to the right bank of the Mekong River up to the border between Kampong Thom and Siem Reap provinces near the Dangrek Mountains, which form the border between Cambodia and Thailand. It was full of hills and mountains as well as vast forests. Transport was difficult, and villages and people were scarce; most were from ethnic minorities. Conditions were tough for our forces, but not complicated for the enemy, which knew the area from when it had previously served as a base. In spite of the difficulties, and confident of popular support, cadres and veterans under our command were determined to push forward.

Before attacking, commanders were assigned to deploy one division for Ratanakkiri, one for Mondulkiri, one for Stung Treng and another for Preah Vihear. The aim was to liberate these provinces quickly and set up revolutionary authorities, to restore security, stability and order while helping people to rebuild their lives. The first target of the offensive, launched on 25 December, was Ratanakkiri. Our forces and Vietnamese soldiers jointly attacked the enemy in Ou Ya Dav. It was taken in the blink of an eye. Many enemy forces were killed while others fled to the road heading to Stung Treng. After the Ou Ya Dav area, we took other districts including Lomphat and Veunsai. By 31 December 1978, Ratanakkiri was free. By the previous day, Kratie Province had been easily taken by a coalition of Front and Vietnamese forces.

In war, nothing is happier than victory. The provinces of Kratie and Ratanakkiri had been set free, the people liberated from the repression, threats and executions of the Pol Pot régime. In December, temperatures fall throughout this region, especially at night; the highlands of Ratanakkiri are so bitterly cold and frosty that people cannot sleep. But following our huge recent victories, cadres and veterans forgot about the cold. The were not worried about the weather or the return of Pol Pot troops. Every unit cheered the enemy's defeat. A new and unforgettable chapter had been opened up in Kratie and Ratanakkiri.

After it was liberated, Ratanakkiri Province became the first support base for the Front in the northeastern region and the temporary headquarters of the General Command, which was aiming to take Mondulkiri Province. This was achieved on 3 January 1979. The defeated enemy forces fled into the forest and moved west.

At the same time, forces liberating Stung Treng Province were pushing forward. The defeated enemy forces from Ratanakkiri were clearly aware of their intentions, and their determination. Since the province was the main military supply base for enemy forces in this region, they had organised their defences in several places. But they had been defeated and their morale was low. Our forces maintained their offensive, and Pol Pot's troops withdrew from the battlefield. By the afternoon of 4 January, Stung Treng was taken, all food warehouses occupied and tonnes of ammunition seized.

It is a long way to Stung Treng from Mondulkiri or Ratanakkiri – even without barriers it takes many hours in a car maintaining a good speed. But the assaults by the Vietnamese military and our forces were like a thunderclap sounding over the country. In 10 days, an extensive area had been taken, and this influenced neighbouring territories.

Between 25 December and 4 January, we took Ratanakkiri, Mondulkiri, Kratie and Stung Treng. These four provinces had a population of about 300,000 and accounted for about a quarter of the country's land area. After Stung Treng, some nearby districts in Preah Vihear Province were also liberated, including Chhaeb and Chey Saen, where the frontline headquarters of the United Front forces was stationed to continue the attacks.

The military campaign to overthrow Pol Pot's Democratic Kampuchea régime, in response to the appeal of the National Salvation Front and the General Command of our forces, was very active not only in the northeast but also in the east, southwest and other regions. In the east, the People's Army of Vietnam defeated the 340th Division, the 305th Division, the 703rd Division and the main base of the 221st Division. Forces in the Eastern Zone of Cambodia and the Seventh Military Region of Vietnam then stormed the remaining enemy forces, liberating Svay Rieng Province on 4 January, Prey Veng Province on 5 January and Kampong Cham Province on 6 January.

In Neak Loeung, enemy positions were manned by Pol Pot troops who had withdrawn from the battlefields of Svay Rieng and Prey Veng. They were ready to resist us on the east and west banks of the Mekong River and blocked us from moving forward. When the forces of the Seventh Military Region of Vietnam and our movement attacked, they put up a strong defence. We defeated the enemy lines on the east bank, but were initially unable to cross the river. Two days later, however, we found a way over to the west bank and dislodged the enemy, allowing our forces to advance to Phnom Penh.

In the southwest, our forces and Vietnamese troops took the main enemy bases with the active support of the people. Between 25 December 1978 and 6 January 1979, the United Front forces and the People's Army of Vietnam defeated the 108th, the 920th, the 805th, the 703rd and the 304th divisions as well as Pol Pot's local army bases in addition to the base of the 221st in the east. Tens of thousands of enemy cadres and fighters surrendered and were taken prisoner. The military apparatus designed to suppress the people had been overthrown. About two thirds of the country's land area and people were now freed and under our control.

Following these defeats, Pol Pot's troops were feeling insecure and losing morale. They did not dare travel on roads or appear in villages. They were afraid of the Vietnamese troops and our forces, and knew that they would be reported if people saw them. So they fled into forests, crossed mountains and gathered in remote areas to hide.

For people liberated from the Pol Pot régime, victory felt like a reincarnation. Everyone who had been evacuated began to return to their villages and support the National Salvation Front. In places that had been partly liberated, the United Front forces gave mandates to people's authorities to reorganise villages, communes, districts, schools and hospitals. We made declarations and distributed propaganda containing statements by the Front so everyone could clearly understand what was happening. We tried to respond to all requests made by the Front and local authorities. It was noticeable that condemnation of the Pol Pot régime, and opposition to its return, were universal. In many areas, people gave tearful accounts of massacres, and demanded justice.

With the military offensive and popular uprising against the Pol Pot régime in full swing, the Third Party Congress was held in Vietnam on 5 January 1979. All generations were there, and so the entire country was represented. I still remember there were four groups – the first led by me with Chea Sim; the second led by Hun Sen; the third led by Pen Sovann, who had been living in northern Vietnam; and the fourth led by Bou Thong, the ethnic minority leader who had fled to Ia Puch Camp in Vietnam. Another group, led by Say Phouthang from the Koh Kong area near the Thai border, was integrated later as it was still operating underground.

The Third Congress refused to acknowledge the congress that Pol Pot and his partisans had convened in the 1960s with the aim of eliminating the Khmer People's Revolutionary Party and declaring the establishment of the Communist Party of Kampuchea. The Third Congress also reorganised the collective leadership of the Khmer People's Revolutionary Party. It condemned Pol Pot, who made the party betray his comrades and take the flesh and blood of its cadres, supporters, the people and international aid to fulfil his ambitions and greed by causing a disaster unprecedented in the history of Cambodia. The congress adopted a political platform to overthrow Pol Pot's régime and restore genuine ownership by the people; create a democratic system; expand Angkorian culture; and transform Cambodia into a peaceful, independent and modern democratic country with good relations and cooperation with foreign countries, regardless of different political systems; and active participation in efforts promoting peace, independence, democracy and development. The congress also decided that the Party had to strengthen its involvement in three main areas – politics, ideology and organisation – by deploying active revolutionary forces, who had been oppressed and attacked by Pol Pot and his followers.

There was an election for a provisional Central Committee of seven leaders – Pen Sovann, myself, Chea Sim, Hun Sen, Bou Thong, Chan Kiri and Vann San. Thus the congress came to an end. It was an historic event to rehabilitate the Khmer People's Revolutionary Party, which in 1991 became known as the Cambodian People's Party (CPP).

Phnom Penh was the régime's last stronghold, although our forces had the advantage. On 5 and 6 January 1979, our forces and Vietnamese troops surrounded the city. However, enemy hardliners refused to surrender, determined to keep fighting. It did not take long for Pol Pot's régime to be overthrown by Vietnamese troops and our forces. Fearing their fate, foreign advisors based in Phnom Penh and senior leaders of the régime, including Pol Pot himself, were evacuated to the west and crossed the border to Thailand.

The revolutionary forces and Vietnamese troops advanced on Phnom Penh simultaneously. They took control of the city on the morning of 7 January. By 12:30 p.m., pockets of resistance had been wiped out. The heart of Cambodia was free. The Pol Pot era was over, and the five-tower flag showing the temples of Angkor was flying proudly over the city.

The victory was accomplished through the blood sacrificed by cadres, soldiers and ordinary Cambodians, supported by our neighbours and other countries around the world. Especially supportive were the state, government, army and people of Vietnam, which provided enormous and effective assistance. Without such efforts, our nation and people would not have won such a victory. The Pol Pot régime, generally acknowledged as one of the most brutal and ferocious in history, could not put up a defence and was overthrown.

The recapture of Phnom Penh on 7 January 1979 greatly excited the people; it was also a morale-booster for the armed forces opposing Pol Pot in other regions. Showing great courage, our forces and Vietnamese volunteer soldiers liberated cities and provinces around the country, including Takeo on 8 January, followed by Kampot, Kampong Speu, Kampong Thom and Kampong Som on 9 January, Siem Reap on 10 January, Kampong Chhnang on 12 January, Battambang on 13 January, Pursat on 14 January, Preah Vihear on 16 January and Koh Kong on 17 January.

Thus, the Pol Pot régime, with all its suffering, terror and murderous threats, came to an end. The date 7 January marked the rebirth of a people who had lived since 1975 in darkness on the brink of almost inevitable death. A new era for Cambodia began, in which the country was owned and controlled by the people. It has continued ever since.

The overthrow of the Pol Pot régime was inevitable as a consequence of its record of killings and oppression. Survivors still remember the bitter suffering they experienced, and will never forget the assistance given by the party, state, government and army of Vietnam and other international friends.* The events of 7 January 1979 represent the defeat of expansionist foreign policies towards Cambodia.

It was an historic starting point, opening an era of independence, freedom and democracy for the nation and the people after the prolonged struggle against imperialism, feudalism, reactionary forces

---

* EDITOR'S NOTE: *Countries providing support to Cambodia after the defeat of the Pol Pot régime were mainly members of the Moscow-based Council for Mutual Economic Assistance (also known as Comecon). Comecon members were Bulgaria, Cuba, Czechoslovakia, East Germany, Hungary, Mongolia, Poland, Romania, the Soviet Union and Vietnam. Additional support came from India and Laos (a Comecon observer).*

and the brutal Pol Pot régime. The priority of the People's Republic of Kampuchea was to play a part in restoring peace and stability across Southeast Asia and the world. We opened a new chapter in international relations, solidarity and cooperation with many countries. Bonds of friendship were established between Cambodia, Vietnam and Laos that had never before existed among the three nations of Indochina.

CHAPTER 6

REBUILDING THE COUNTRY

As we have seen, Cambodia and her people were liberated from Pol Pot's régime on 7 January 1979, an historic event followed by the conclusion of the Third Congress of the Khmer People's Revolutionary Party. In Phnom Penh on 8 January, the People's Republic of Kampuchea established the People's Revolutionary Council with eight members. I chaired the council while Pen Sovann served as Vice Chairman and Minister of National Defence. The other members were Chea Sim (Minister of Interior), Hun Sen (Minister of Foreign Affairs), Nou Beng (Minister of Public Health), Chan Ven (Minister of Education), Keo Chenda (Minister of Propaganda, Information and Culture) and Mok Sakun (Minister of Industry and Chairman of the Committee on Economy and Livelihoods). 'Pol Pot's dictatorial fascist régime has been totally abolished,' the council announced. 'From now on, the new order is the People's Republic of Kampuchea, the only legitimate representative of the people of Cambodia. The practices of the People's Revolutionary Council shall lead the people in applying without fail the 11-point programme defined in the statement adopted by the United Front for the National Salvation of Kampuchea on December 2, 1978.'

The announcement had a marked impact throughout the country

and across the world. The Socialist Republic of Vietnam became the first state to give diplomatic recognition to the People's Republic of Kampuchea as the legitimate representative of the country on 9 January. Others followed, including Laos, the Soviet Union, the German Democratic Republic, Hungary, Poland, Bulgaria, Czechoslovakia, Cuba, Mongolia, Afghanistan, Nicaragua, India and Ethiopia. With diplomatic recognition came the establishment of foreign embassies, which enhanced the reputation of the new administration. The People's Republic of Kampuchea was the first state genuinely representing workers and farmers ever seen in the history of Cambodia. It truly represented Cambodian interests.

The priority was now to ensure stability and people's livelihoods. Both the authorities and the people had been left empty-handed. Production and technical facilities had been destroyed. So too had schools, hospitals, temples, towns and cities, markets, trade, currency, commercial products and traffic. The workforce had crumbled. In short, the economic infrastructure had melted away. Gone, too, were many of the nation's cultural and other traditions.

In 1979, foreign observers were describing Cambodia as a 'graveyard' in the aftermath of 'Year Zero'. The experiment in social change carried out by the Pol Pot-Ieng Sary régime had meant three years, eight months and twenty days of blood and tears, bringing Cambodia to the brink. 'All towns and cities are seen as a sequence of events in a nightmare,' was one description. 'They feel as if they are living in a city shortly after it is destroyed by a nuclear bomb.' It was a society of nothingness in turmoil and total chaos, with a severe threat of a disastrous famine.

After abandoning the collectives set up by Pol Pot, families were going hungry. Others were returning with nothing from where they had been evacuated. As Pol Pot's forces withdrew, they had torched rice left in warehouses and paddy fields. Food was scarce across the country. Never in history had our people had such a terrible experience. Although we had escaped from the abyss of death, we now faced severe famine. Despite having plenty of food today, older Cambodians never forget this horrific period in which we desperately looked for things to eat in order to survive. The authorities appealed to other countries and charities worldwide for urgent assistance. A few days later, Vietnam, the Soviet Union and several international agencies responded to the appeal by donating tens of thousands of tonnes of rice (according to the Central Food Company, Soviet food aid included 70,557 tonnes of rice in 1979 and Vietnam provided a further 140,000 tonnes). Because of this humanitarian aid, our people were gradually saved from disaster and standards of living improved.

In 1979, the People's Revolutionary Council faced what seemed like overwhelming difficulties. Under the supervision of cadres delegated by the Central Committee of the Party, institutions were set up at the national and provincial levels. We then established people's revolutionary committees in the provinces and towns. At the district level, we had no cadres delegated by the Central Committee, so we nominated local people who had suffered under the Pol Pot régime and joined with our revolutionary forces in establishing control over the districts. They formed people's revolutionary committees at the district level. In communes and villages, revolutionary committees were elected by the people. Thus, authorities were set up at all levels to help restore and improve people's livelihoods. At the same time, we began training courses to guide the politics and ideology of the revolutionary cadres.

As a matter of urgency, we paid great attention to building up the armed forces – the defeat of the enemy was still fresh. This was a core mission, an immediate requirement. We lacked officers to consolidate our achievements. At the time of victory, we had more than 200 cadres, but most were completely inexperienced in terms of leadership and management. So we did our best to attract and recruit experienced officials from the previous régime, and other educated people, providing ideological training before sending them back to work. We were constantly striving to develop technicians with short training courses. We soon managed to overcome the shortage of cadres and technicians who would take responsibility for their new roles.

We had no more than 30 battalions – not enough troops to maintain our victory. So after Pol Pot fled, Vietnamese troops continued to assist Cambodia's revolution while we made every effort to build up our own armed forces. Eventually, we formed the Khmer People's Revolutionary Armed Forces, consisting of front-line soldiers, regional troops and militia as well as air and naval forces. The Revolutionary Armed Forces grew in size: the aim was gradually to replace the Vietnamese Voluntary Army in Kampuchea. Meanwhile the forces of the Pol Pot régime were either hiding in mountains or had been forced to flee to Thailand.

As the wet season approached in 1979, we tried to provide farmers with seed. So that they could support one another, we applied collective principles and gathered farmers into groups of 10–15 households. People helped one other to ensure that assistance went to the elderly, the disabled and orphans. Although we lacked farm tools and manpower, these challenges were gradually overcome. Despite the difficulties of that first year, we still managed to plant more than 770,000 hectares and harvest an estimated 265,220 tonnes of rice. It was a small crop. Yet despite the absence of ploughs and draft animals and the shortage of seed, we were motivated. We had hoes and shovels. The quantities harvested were remarkable, given the scarcity of food and other difficulties.

With efforts by all sectors of the population, and support from neighbouring countries and others around the world, in 1979 we overcame the severe famine. Livelihoods gradually started to recover. Markets, long since abolished by Pol Pot, were restored. Instead of cash, people bartered rice and gold or precious gems they had hidden. This was new, and illustrated how Cambodian society was evolving after being freed from Pol Pot's inhumane régime.

The economy and other aspects of society quickly recovered. A notable advance came on 20 March 1980, when we reversed the abolition of currency by issuing riel bank notes for people to use in their daily lives and to enable us to be economically compatible with the rest of the world.

The industrial sector lay in ruins. There were few skilled workers and most factories and other enterprises had either been demolished or left idle. Among 100 small- and large-scale manufacturing facilities, only those that still had raw materials were operating after the establishment of the Ministry of Industry and the Committee on Economy and Livelihoods. Electricity and water supplies were restored in Phnom Penh around the middle of January 1979.

After cadres, manual workers and former skilled labourers at factories and enterprises returned home, they put all their efforts, without complaint, into reviving economic activity and rebuilding the foundations of industrial production. Despite inexperienced management and lack of planning, the restored factories and enterprises increased in number from 34 to 61, and the total value of production in 1979 was estimated as equivalent to around 139 million riel.

The overall economy was small. But starting from nothing was symbolic. The restoration of industry had political benefits and provided consumer goods to people who were otherwise unable to make ends meet. The Cambodian revolution was changing rapidly and further economic growth was required. On 27 November 1979, the Ministry of Economy and Livelihoods was founded. By this stage, the recovery in manufacturing was in full swing and gradually becoming better organised.

Perhaps no other country in world history could have made such progress. The country had been destroyed. After the defeat of the Pol Pot régime, we were empty handed; but the people, cadres and authorities were all determined to address all the various challenges they faced.

Education and cultural activity had been abolished by the Pol Pot régime. Few qualified teachers survived. Schools and other educational institutions were left silent and in poor condition. Literature, art, poetry, cinema, theatre, music and reading had been reduced to a minimum and in some cases completely lost. So after Liberation, we had to fully revive education and culture.

When the 1979–1980 school year opened, we focused on teacher training, expanding the number of primary schools and eliminating illiteracy, which was widespread across the country. With the support of friendly neighbours and other countries, as well as international agencies and the constant effort of all authorities, cadres and teachers who had previous experience, we shaped an education system. In the first year, we had 947,307 students enrolled in 17,861 classes in 5,290 primary schools in addition to 8,229 children in 230 kindergarten classes. We also had 4,803 students in 101 classes at 14 junior high schools and 281 students in seven classes at a senior high school. During that first year, we had 26,019 teachers. They were precious assets at the time.

Our efforts to combat illiteracy met with considerable success.

The Summary Report on the Evaluation of the Results of the Literacy Campaign in 1980 estimated the number of illiterate people at 1,362,354. We started to combat illiteracy on 15 June 1979. Before we even launched the National Illiteracy Fighting Day, we had 61,242 students with 1,365 classes and 1,516 teachers throughout the country.

On the cultural front, we did our best to gather actors and actresses who had survived the Pol Pot régime. In 1979 and 1980, a total of 362 former performing artists resumed work. We restructured cultural management at all levels and collected cultural properties that had either been destroyed or abandoned by the régime. We tried to restore the arts both centrally and at the commune level to preserve cultural properties and items of national heritage.

In the following years, important cultural activities were gradually restored by our cadres, actors, actresses and artists. We set up 41 troupes of professional actors and actresses, 2,950 bands of popular artists and 60 mobile theatres. We also started training courses for dancers. We revived the Buddhist monkhood and temples as well as national traditions such as weddings and ritual ceremonies, which had been destroyed by the Pol Pot régime. After Liberation, people were delighted to be able once again to celebrate weddings for their children and hold religious ceremonies.

The rebirth of culture and artists in particular not only entertained audiences and influenced politics but also played a major role in bringing the country back to life.

The health sector was the focus of great attention. Following the establishment of the People's Revolutionary Council in early January 1979, the Ministry of Public Health and Social Affairs was set up with fewer than 50 doctors and only 20 pharmacists. However, with support from Vietnam and international humanitarian agencies, we were able gradually to develop the ministry and pay more attention to reviving, building and expanding health facilities. By the end of 1979, we were able to restore as many as 605 treatment centres across the country – three at the central level, 11 at the municipal or provincial level, 107 at the district level and 484 at the commune level with 7,575 beds in total.

At the same time, we put great effort into gathering former health workers, medical students, pharmacists and doctors, training them in political ideology before assigning them to different treatment centres. We were able to get some of them back to work. However, these efforts were not sufficient, as so few health workers had survived the Pol Pot régime. Though we faced a lot of difficulties, we tried our best to provide short-course training to the health workers. Under local leaders, health boards were set up at the provincial, district and commune levels. Health services expanded rapidly and improved.

After Pol Pot fled west, people who had been forcibly evacuated or detained behind bars returned to their villages one way or another, many with chronic diseases. The expansion of health facilities at all levels meant that people were treated on time. While we faced many challenges after Liberation, our new revolutionary authorities and soldiers, supported by many countries, some of them our friendly neighbours and others further afield, the health sector continued to progress in subsequent years.

CHAPTER 7

THE INTERNATIONAL DIMENSION

To make foreign countries aware of the situation in Cambodia and strengthen bilateral ties, much attention was paid to international relations after Liberation. During a visit by Vietnamese Prime Minister Pham Van Dong to Cambodia on 18 February 1979, I signed the Treaty of Peace, Friendship and Cooperation between our two countries. The essence of the treaty was peaceful coexistence, respect for mutual sovereignty and national independence, non-interference in each other's internal affairs, equality and mutual benefits. It was an historic and fruitful visit followed in March with a visit by a Lao delegation led by Comrade Souphanouvong, the head of state. I signed a treaty between the People's Republic of Kampuchea and the Lao People's Democratic Republic, which was of similar significance to the one with the Socialist Republic of Vietnam.

Such a degree of friendship and cooperation between the Cambodian, Vietnamese and Lao peoples had never happened before and was greatly strengthened and expanded. The population of all three countries greeted these developments with enthusiasm. They were determined to maintain and protect this solidarity, constantly on the alert for any destructive moves by our enemies.

Exchanges of official visits and signing agreements between our new administration and friendly countries after Liberation greatly facilitated the expansion of external relations and cooperation. As senior party and state delegations made official visits to countries in Asia, Europe, Africa and Latin America, respect for the People's Republic of Kampuchea grew internationally.

The rebirth of the Cambodian people required enormous sacrifices, and great effort in overcoming innumerable obstacles. The struggle by our cadres, soldiers and citizens to rebuild Cambodia is still with us. We were assisted by near and distant friends, international agencies, people from developed nations and especially the priceless, honest and direct support from Vietnam. Of course, we faced obstacles and difficulties after Liberation just like any country that had been plunged into disaster. The devastation suffered by countries in World War II, however, cannot truly be compared with the catastrophe in Cambodia under Pol Pot's administration. The other party leaders and I tried to restore stability and people's living standards, setting up administrative structures from the top down to the grassroots level, and rebuilding the military and Party structures. After the second session of the Fourth Congress of the Central Committee of the Party agreed to dismiss Pen Sovann as secretary-general, as the new secretary-general I tried to expand the Party's top echelons. By February 1985, we had 6,000 partisans and a core of 3,895 groups with 28,600 members as forces to expand the party. Party branches were now located in 127 of the country's 139 districts.

Between 13 and 16 October 1985, I chaired the Fifth Party Congress, at which we approved economic reforms and social welfare measures that would be implemented between 1986 and 1990.

The congress elected a new Central Committee with 45 members including 14 reserve members. I was re-elected as secretary-general among 11 members who were elected to the Politburo including two reserve members and five permanent members.

From 5 to 12 April 1989, I chaired a national congress of cadres which decided to have the remaining Vietnamese volunteer troops withdrawn from Cambodia. The congress adopted policies for private transport and agriculture as well as small industries and handicrafts within the framework of the collective, private and state economies. We also adopted policies on land management, industrial production, natural resources and farm labour.

At the end of my tenure as secretary-general of the Party, I chaired an Extraordinary Congress on 17 and 18 October 1991. We decided to change the name of the Khmer People's Revolutionary Party to the Cambodian People's Party (CPP). Under the change, members of the Politburo became members of a new Permanent Committee of the Central Committee of the CPP and members of the Central Secretariat were moved to a Standing Central Committee. Chea Sim was elected chairman of the newly formed CPP with Hun Sen elected as deputy chairman. I was elected as honorary chairman.

While the Cambodian people were looking forward to opening a new page in our country's history, Pol Pot was given asylum and land by the Thai government. After escaping to the Thai border in 1979, his forces had strengthened their numbers and built several bases in Thailand along Cambodia's western border. They took people they captured and others to set up refugee camps, hiding their presence from the public. They received constant international support from unfriendly forces. After 7 January 1979, Funcinpec (Front uni national pour un Cambodge indépendant, neutre, pacifique, et cooperative), Moulinaka (Mouvement pour la libération nationale du Kampuchéa) and Son Sann's party emerged to fight against the Phnom Penh government. With moral and material support from several countries, the leaders of these groups used both political and military tactics to overthrow the young government in Cambodia. However, with the backing of the Cambodian people we were determined to do our utmost to defend and preserve the power of the revolutionary state, and fight back on all fronts. Our new government was expanding and getting stronger as it gained experience.

In August 1979, the People's Revolutionary Court in Phnom Penh sentenced senior leaders Pol Pot and Ieng Sary to death *in absentia*. Six hundred representatives of victims took part, along with 50 international guests and lawyers. Despite being condemned by public opinion, opposition forces based along the border agreed to set up a tripartite 'Coalition Government of Democratic Kampuchea' in Kuala Lumpur in 1982 to oppose the Cambodian people who supported our new government. They tried every tactic – including military force – to overthrow our young revolution. They accused us of having Vietnamese forces in Cambodia. But when the Vietnamese withdrew, they would not accept the facts in their continued propaganda. They constantly whipped up popular anger towards Vietnam to make it easier to overthrow us. Pol Pot's forces continued the genocidal killings they had practised from 1975 to early 1979. Their propaganda was a means of gathering strength, with no relationship to reality. With our own experience of the Pol Pot régime, realisation of this fact motivated us in our struggle to protect our new state, to defend our livelihoods, and to prevent a return of the bloody genocidal régime – without any compromises and by all means necessary.

After the Vietnamese forces returned home, fighting seemed to increase, especially along the Cambodia-Thai border. The People's

Republic of Kampuchea, later renamed the State of Cambodia, continued to maintain strong defences. In the Politburo of the Khmer People's Revolutionary Party, however, there was a wish to end the bloodshed between Cambodians. As Secretary-General, I decided to delegate Hun Sen, as representative of the Party and chairman of the Council of Ministers, to attend a first meeting in Paris on 2 December 1987, with Prince Norodom Sihanouk, the exiled prince who had been serving as the president of the Coalition Government of Democratic Kampuchea. Subsequent meetings between Hun Sen and Prince Sihanouk took place in Paris, Jakarta, Tokyo and Pattaya with the aim of seeking a political settlement of the Cambodian conflict.

After the first session of an international conference co-chaired by France and Indonesia in Paris between 30 July and 30 August 1989, the two sides agreed to form a Supreme National Council (SNC). Set up in September 1990, the council had 12 members. Six were from the State of Cambodia. The rest were from the tripartite resistance including Funcinpec, headed by Prince Norodom Ranariddh in the place of his father, who was now neutral. The SNC had its first meeting in Bangkok and held another five meetings in Paris, New York, Jakarta, Pattaya and Beijing. The meeting agreed to appoint Prince Sihanouk as chair of the SNC.

At the second session of the international conference in France from 21 to 23 October 1991, the four parties – the State of Cambodia, Funcinpec, Son Sann's party and the Party of Democratic Kampuchea (the Khmer Rouge) – signed the Paris Peace Agreements in the name of Prince Sihanouk in his capacity as chairman of the Supreme National Council. The first agreement was related to sovereignty, territorial integrity, neutrality and national independence; and the second was a declaration on the rehabilitation and reconstruction of Cambodia. Eighteen other countries took part in the conference, namely Australia, Brunei Darussalam, Canada, China, France, India, Japan, the Lao People's Democratic Republic, Malaysia, Indonesia, the Philippines, Singapore, the Soviet Union, Thailand, the United Kingdom, the United States and Vietnam – as well as Yugoslavia in its capacity as chair of the Non-Aligned Movement. The United Nations Secretary-General also took part.

CHAPTER 8

A NEW CONSTITUTION

The Paris Peace Agreements stated that the Supreme National Council was the only legal body that would control transitional sovereignty and national unity. All council members pledged to hold free and fair elections for a new government. The council, however, had to transfer temporary power to a United Nations Advance Mission in Cambodia to guarantee implementation of the agreement, organise elections and govern the war-torn country. To ensure political neutrality, the UN mission had to inspect or manage a number of major ministries such as the Ministry of National Defence, the Ministry of Finance, the Ministry of Interior and the Ministry of Information.

The peace agreements required a ceasefire, regroupment of military forces and reductions in troop levels as well as the confiscation of all kinds of weapons from the adversaries. The United Nations was responsible for the return of 360,000 refugees from the Cambodia-Thai border as well as helping them reintegrate into society and cast ballots in a multiparty election.

A few days after the UN mission started operating, on 14 November 1991, Prince Sihanouk returned to Cambodia. With him on the flight from Beijing was his wife Princess Monineath and Council of Ministers Chairman Hun Sen.

The members of the tripartite resistance Coalition Government of Democratic Kampuchea had their headquarters in Phnom Penh and were protected by local authorities and UN peacekeeping forces. The first meeting of the Supreme National Council on Cambodian soil took place on 30 December 1991, with all 12 members taking part, including Khieu Samphan and Son Sen from the Party of Democratic Kampuchea. The Khmer Rouge, however, abused the peace agreements by violating the ceasefire and not allowing the United Nations Transitional Authority in Cambodia (UNTAC) to inspect the area it controlled, in the northwest along the Cambodia-Thai border. Khmer Rouge forces intensified their political and military struggle, including acts of terrorism. Eight months after the signing of the Paris Peace Agreements, clashes escalated in the provinces of Preah Vihear, Kampong Thom and Kampong Cham. Guerrilla warfare also took place in the provinces of Kampong Speu, Takeo and Kampot.

Despite a Khmer Rouge boycott, the UN was determined to proceed with the deployment of 15,000 military personnel and 5,000 civil servants from 30 countries at an estimated cost of $2 billion. Its goal was to see free and fair elections and the formation of a new government recognised by the international community. The UN set 23 May 1993 for the Cambodian elections under a proportional system, and registered more than four million potential voters aged 18 years and upwards. There were 3,268 candidates from 20 political parties, including 240 from the Cambodian People's Party, 240 from Funcinpec, and 238 from the Buddhist Liberal Democratic Party of Son Sann. The Khmer Rouge did not let UNTAC or rival political parties enter the territories they occupied. In the areas under the control of the State of Cambodia, however, UN forces and the political parties were allowed to exercise their full freedoms. The Cambodian people cast their ballots between 23 and 28 May. With

4,011,331 registered voters, 89.55 per cent of the votes were valid; 118,745 votes or just under 3 per cent were invalid; and the rest did not turn out to vote.

Only four parties won enough votes to qualify for the 120-seat National Assembly. Funcinpec obtained 45.47 per cent of the vote amounting to 58 seats, followed by the Cambodian People's Party with 38.22 per cent (51 seats), the Buddhist Liberal Democratic Party with 3.81 per cent (10 seats) and Moulinaka with 1.37 per cent (1 seat). On 10 June, UNTAC chief Yasushi Akashi announced the results, describing the elections as free and fair. Funcinpec and the Buddhist Liberal Democratic Party accepted the results; and Reginald Austin, head of UNTAC's electoral component, announced that 120 members of parliament had been elected (including myself in Kandal Province).

The CPP declared that the election results had many irregularities. A statement by Hun Sen before the Supreme National Council was the main point of conflict between the CPP and UNTAC. The dispute had been going on since the beginning of the election campaign. The CPP's official complaint accused UNTAC of lacking neutrality, amending the election law without consulting the Supreme National Council, and preventing representatives of political parties from inspecting places where ballot boxes were kept at night (it was found that some locks for ballot boxes were broken and several boxes were empty). Instances of people voting several times were also found at many locations.

On 11 June, senior Khmer Rouge leader Khieu Samphan made a statement appealing for the top six CPP leaders to be assassinated. Funcinpec and the Buddhist Liberal Democratic Party meanwhile announced a coalition giving the two parties 68 seats in the 120-seat National Assembly.

Three days later, a constituent assembly convened its first session and approved a proposal by Funcinpec, the CPP and the Buddhist Liberal Democrats. The decision reversed the parliamentary vote which had overthrown Prince Sihanouk on 18 March 1970, and returned him to power as head of state. The constituent assembly had three months to draft, discuss and approve a new constitution.

On 15 June, the UN Security Council adopted Resolution 840 recognising the election result. A day later, the Royal Palace declared that Prince Sihanouk had appointed his son Prince Norodom Ranariddh and Hun Sen as co-prime ministers of a provisional government of Cambodia, tasking them with forming a cabinet (Council of Ministers) to be approved by the new National Assembly.

On 24 September, the new constitution came into effect forming the Kingdom of Cambodia as a constitutional monarchy with Norodom Sihanouk resuming his positions as king and head of state. At the same time, Chea Sim became president of the National Assembly, Loy Sim Chheang (Funcinpec) became the assembly's first vice president and Son Soubert (Buddhist Liberal Democratic Party) became second vice president.

The king reappointed Prince Ranariddh as first prime minister and Hun Sen as second prime minister. In the spirit of national reconciliation, the new coalition government had two deputy prime ministers – Sar Kheng (CPP) and Ing Kiet (Funcinpec). The two parties shared equal power in 24 ministries and state secretariats. Two positions of secretary of state, which could be in any of the ministries, were reserved for the Buddhist Liberal Democratic Party and Moulinaka. All the parties that gained seats in the National Assembly were represented in the coalition government – there was no opposition. The two main parties shared provincial governor and deputy governor positions as well as the posts of municipal mayor and deputy mayor. Armed forces were integrated into the new Royal Cambodian Armed Forces and the National Police with the two co-prime ministers as joint commanders-in-chief.

The Kingdom of Cambodia had a policy of good relations and active cooperation in all fields with neighbouring and other countries. Today it has diplomatic relations with more than 100 countries, with dozens of ambassadors accredited to Phnom Penh.

Japan and France coordinated aid to Cambodia through the International Conference on the Rehabilitation and Reconstruction of Cambodia, which met every year alternately in Japan and France. International assistance of about $700 million a year came from some 40 countries and agencies that took part in the process after it was launched in 1992. By 1996, private and public inflows into Cambodia had reached about $2 billion. Almost 20 banks were operating in Phnom Penh and the provinces, the annual inflation rate had dropped from 150 per cent to less than 4 per cent, and the local currency was stable. New roads, bridges, hospitals, schools and irrigation systems were inaugurated along with hotels and resorts.

Yet Cambodia still faced internal problems: the Khmer Rouge were refusing to honour the Paris Peace Agreements. They had not only boycotted the election but also continued to rule their autonomous zones, using force to attack the government and people in remote areas. On 7 July 1994, the National Assembly passed legislation to outlaw the Khmer Rouge. The legislation aimed to pressure the Khmer Rouge in terms of the spirit of the law; the intention was to make the public aware that the Khmer Rouge forces were outlawed guerrillas, unable to comply with the peace agreements, who could not escape accountability for the atrocities committed during Pol Pot's rule from 1975 to 1978. Without question, they had to be brought to justice.

During the dry season in 1994 and 1995, government forces attacked and briefly occupied the main Khmer Rouge bases in areas along the Thai border such as Pailin and Anlong Veng and then withdrew following an appeal from the king. Although the Khmer Rouge had been outlawed, the Royal Government offered amnesties to those low-ranking officers and soldiers who defected from the Khmer Rouge political organisation and joined with the government.

Thus, the use of force to solve the Khmer Rouge problem was blocked by the intervention of the king. The Royal Cambodian Armed Forces were made up of elements of both Funcinpec and CPP. In an arrogant move, His Royal Highness Norodom Ranariddh sought to upset this careful balance. With the aim of overthrowing the CPP, His Royal Highness proposed to confront his party's partner in the coalition government during a seminar in Sihanoukville in 1996, which led to armed clashes on 5–6 July 1997 that destabilised the country.

'The Royal Coalition Government is only a slogan, its real meaning is an empty basket,' His Royal Highness said. Moreover, he claimed, 'the current royal coalition government is a Vietnamese puppet royal government,' even though half its members were from Funcinpec.

At a party congress, he openly threatened the country with political instability. 'Funcinpec must withdraw from the coalition government and the National Assembly,' he said, indicating that the government would be dissolved for early elections. His reasoning was unclear. 'The CPP did not share power with Funcinpec at the district level,' he claimed.

In fact, the Paris Peace Agreements had not mentioned power sharing at the district level. However, Deputy Prime Minister Sar Kheng, who was also the co-Minister of Interior from the CPP, was already making district power sharing arrangements under a directive from Second Prime Minister Hun Sen and was waiting for a list of names from Funcinpec. You Hockry, the co-Minister of Interior from Funcinpec, admitted that the list was late.

Following the misplaced accusation by Prince Ranariddh, the CPP announced a halt to sharing power at the district level – since it was not mentioned in the peace accords – and its intention to continue running the government and upholding the constitution. By this stage, Funcinpec was in disarray, beset by insoluble internal disputes.

Aiming to overthrow the CPP and seize power, Prince Ranariddh and some of the generals loyal to him made secret contact with Pol Pot in Anlong Veng in 1997 to unite Funcinpec forces with the Khmer Rouge forces, so as to achieve a so-called strategic military balance. The allied forces were to be brought into Phnom Penh to destroy the CPP partners in the coalition government. The pretext was to let Pol Pot's forces play a legal military and political role in society, supposedly to end the war and bring full peace to the country. The real motive was to use Pol Pot's forces to strengthen those of Funcinpec.

After numerous rounds of secret communications, Prince Ranariddh ordered his generals to bring some of Pol Pot's forces from Anlong Veng into the outskirts of Phnom Penh. This intensified the situation, forcing a special coalition committee to deal with the irregularities of the Royal Government. These ambitions of the prince and Funcinpec prompted the armed clashes on 5–6 July 1997, which lasted about 20 hours. Before the fighting erupted, Prince Ranariddh had sneaked out of the country. He went into exile and was later sentenced to prison *in absentia*.

After defeating the insurgent forces, Second Prime Minister Hun Sen announced the government's commitment always to act in accordance with the constitution, the National Assembly, royal executive bodies and the civil service. Prince Ranariddh and his followers would face the law. The chief of general staff of the Royal Cambodian Armed Forces and the General Commissariat of National Police at the Ministry of Interior subsequently seized 15,676 weapons and a large quantity of other military supplies, matériel and equipment from the rebel forces around Phnom Penh and military garrisons in provinces and towns around the country. The government meanwhile set up a coalition investigative committee to look into compensation for companies and individuals who had lost property during the clashes. Industry, commerce, banking, investment and tourism gradually resumed. So did foreign aid, notwithstanding a suspension by the United States.

After a seven-month deadlock at the National Assembly, things returned to normal with the opening of the Eighth Plenary Session of the First Legislature on 28 July. On the morning of 6 August, 98 members of parliament out of the 99 present voted to remove the parliamentary immunity of Prince Ranariddh. To replace him, Foreign Minister Ung Huot was elected First Prime Minister with 86 votes, exceeding the two-thirds majority required. Countries with diplomatic relations with Cambodia considered the events as an internal affair.

As elections approached in 1998, King Sihanouk pardoned Prince Ranariddh. He returned from exile and was elected as a lawmaker from Kampong Cham Province, ultimately becoming president of the National Assembly. At the same time, after the 1998 elections Cambodia followed other countries in having a single prime minister and united armed forces.

Pol Pot's forces did not take part in the elections and still occupied several areas, especially in Anlong Veng and Pailin. On behalf of the top leadership of the CPP, Prime Minister Hun Sen announced a 'win-win' policy, sending agents to secretly contact Pol Pot's remaining forces and persuade them to defect to the government. By the end of 1998, the protracted civil war was finally over. For the first time in centuries, Cambodia was at peace. In accordance with the heartfelt wishes of the Cambodian people and the desires of many other countries, the hardline masterminds of the Khmer Rouge régime – Nuon Chea, Khieu Samphan, Ieng Sary, Ieng Thirith and Duch – were detained in 2007, and in due course put on trial for crimes against humanity, genocide and war crimes at the hybrid Extraordinary Chambers in the Courts of Cambodia. Thus closed the darkest chapter in our history. It had lasted for decades.

In extinguishing the fire of war – something the UN was unable to achieve – Cambodians and observers from other nations expressed admiration for the tactics of the CPP leaders, especially Prime Minister Hun Sen. Since that time, Cambodians have been living peacefully without territorial divisions. The people are protected by the constitution. They have freedom of expression, religious belief and movement – and the right to establish political parties, non-governmental organisations and other associations. At the time of writing, Cambodia has more than 3,000 NGOs, 101 radio stations, 13 television channels and about 400 newspapers and magazines.

In the election of 27 July 1998, I was elected as a lawmaker from Kampong Cham Province and subsequently first vice president of the National Assembly. During the course of the Second Legislature, we passed 88 laws. I was re-elected from Kampong Cham in the next election, on 27 July 2003. However, it took almost a year to form a new government. Funcinpec was conspiring with the Sam Rainsy Party to set up an alliance; the Cambodian People's Party alone could not form a government, which required a two-thirds majority. At the First Plenary Session of the Third Legislature on 15 December,

Samdech Chea Sim and His Excellency Chea Soth (respectively, the President of the Senate and the oldest member of the National Assembly) validated the new lawmakers who took their oaths the same day. Only CPP lawmakers attended. To ensure political stability, we tried to end the deadlock through negotiations with Funcinpec which eventually abandoned its alliance with the Sam Rainsy Party to form a coalition with the CPP.

At a plenary session of the National Assembly chaired by Chea Soth on 8 July 2004, a total of 96 of the 123 members of parliament approved a constitutional amendment to ensure the regular functioning of national institutions. The new law stipulated procedures for voting by the majority political party to elect the National Assembly's president and vice presidents as well as the chairs and vice chairs of its commissions. After the new law was promulgated by Royal Decree (NS/RKM/0704/001) on 13 July, a National Assembly session chaired by Chea Soth elected the president and vice-presidents along with the commission chairs and vice chairs. All 96 members of parliament who voted supported the amendment. Prince Ranariddh was elected as president of the new assembly; I was elected first vice president; and His Excellency Nguon Nhel (CPP) was elected second vice president.

Having seen how Funcinpec had jeopardised the constitution and risked plunging the country into crisis and political instability, Samdech Hun Sen, Samdech Chea Sim and I decided that we had to amend the constitutional requirement, in the formation of a government, from a two-thirds majority to an absolute majority (50 per cent plus one). This measure reflected the thinking of Samdech Hun Sen, and the Sam Rainsy Party joined with the CPP in supporting the constitutional amendment.

At the Fourth Plenary Session of the Third Legislature on 2 March

2006, a total of 96 of the 97 members of the National Assembly present voted to approve amendments to the constitution (Articles 82, 88, 90, 98, 106, 111 and 114 along with six articles of the Additional Constitutional Law). The amendments were promulgated by Royal Decree (NS/RKM/0306/006) on 9 March.

A day after the vote to amend the constitution, Prince Ranariddh resigned as president of the National Assembly. On 21 March, I was unanimously elected as the new president, with 112 votes. Nguon Nhel was elected first vice president and His Excellency Hong Sun Huot (Funcinpec) was elected second vice president to succeed His Excellency You Hockry. In my term as speaker for the Third Legislature, we passed 145 laws. I led Cambodia's parliamentary delegations to the general assemblies of the ASEAN Inter-Parliamentary Assembly (AIPA) in Cebu in 2006 and Kuala Lumpur in 2007 as well as an extraordinary meeting of the AIPA Executive Committee, which was held in the Malaysian capital the same year.

At the next general election on 27 July 2008, I was re-elected as a member of parliament in Kampong Cham constituency. The First Plenary Session of the Fourth Legislature was presided over by His Majesty King Norodom Sihamoni at the new National Assembly building on 24 September. As the oldest member of parliament, Chea Soth confirmed the validity of the 119 members present who were sworn in the same day. Chea Soth also presided over my re-election as president of the National Assembly. Nguon Nhel was re-elected first vice president and His Excellency Say Chhum was elected second vice president. During my term as speaker for the Fourth Legislature, we passed 94 laws.

After becoming speaker, I also led our delegations to three general assemblies of the Inter-Parliamentary Union (IPU) in Nairobi in 2006, Bali in 2007 and Cape Town in 2008. In addition, I led the Cambodian delegations to annual meetings of the Asia-Pacific Parliamentary Forum (APPF) in Moscow in 2007 and Auckland in 2008.

With Cambodia assuming the chairmanship of the ASEAN Inter-Parliamentary Assembly (AIPA) in 2010, I had the honour of serving as AIPA president for one year, chairing the Thirty-Second General Assembly of AIPA in Phnom Penh in 2011 and leading the Cambodian parliamentary delegation to a meeting with government leaders at the Eighteenth ASEAN Summit in Jakarta. I also led our parliamentary delegations to AIPA general assemblies in Singapore in 2008, Pattaya in 2009, Hanoi in 2010 and Lombok in 2012 as well as the IPU general assemblies in Addis Ababa in 2009, Panama City in 2011 and Quebec City in 2012. In addition, I represented Cambodia at the Third World Conference of Speakers of Parliament in Geneva in 2010 and led our parliamentary delegations to Asia-Pacific Parliamentary Forum annual meetings in Vientiane in 2009, Singapore in 2010, Ulaanbaatar in 2011 and Tokyo in 2012.

CHAPTER 9

FOCUS ON DEVELOPMENT

Following the collapse of the genocidal Pol Pot régime and the end of the civil war, I focused my efforts on improving legislation that would lead the country towards development. Cambodia not only regained its seat at the United Nations (previously held by the Khmer Rouge) but contributed its own troops to UN peacekeeping forces in countries such as the Central African Republic, Lebanon, South Sudan, Sudan and Syria. In Hanoi, on 30 April 1999, Cambodia became a member of the Association of Southeast Asian Nations and held the one-year rotating chairmanship of ASEAN in 2002 and 2012. Cambodia became a member of the World Trade Organization (WTO) on 19 September 2003.

By 2011, the annual rate of economic growth was 7.1 per cent and the riel had strengthened against the dollar – despite the abuse of our sovereign territory by the Thai military and devastating floods. GDP per capita was $909 and would increase to an estimated $1,000 as soon as 2013. The area covered by rice fields had expanded by more than six per cent from a year earlier to 2.97 million hectares yielding 9.3 million tonnes, including a surplus of 3.03 million tonnes to be kept as reserves. The unprecedented increase in agricultural production led the Royal Government to forecast that an-

Assuming the two-year rotating presidency of the Asian Parliamentary Assembly (APA) from Pakistan's Senate Chairman Raza Rabbani (left) at the assembly's Eighth Plenary Session in Phnom Penh in 2015 with National Assembly Second Vice President Nguon Nhel (right)

(Left and below) Addressing the Eighth Plenary Session of the Asian Parliamentary Assembly (APA). Founded during the Seventh General Assembly of the Association of Asian Parliaments for Peace (AAPP) in Tehran in 2006, APA now has more than 40 member parliaments. In addition to holding the APA presidency between 2015 and 2017, Cambodia hosted the Second General Assembly of AAPP in Phnom Penh in 2000 following the First General Assembly in Dhaka in 1999.

His Majesty King Norodom Sihamoni presiding over the oath-taking ceremony for newly elected members of parliament at the Royal Palace in Phnom Penh, 2013

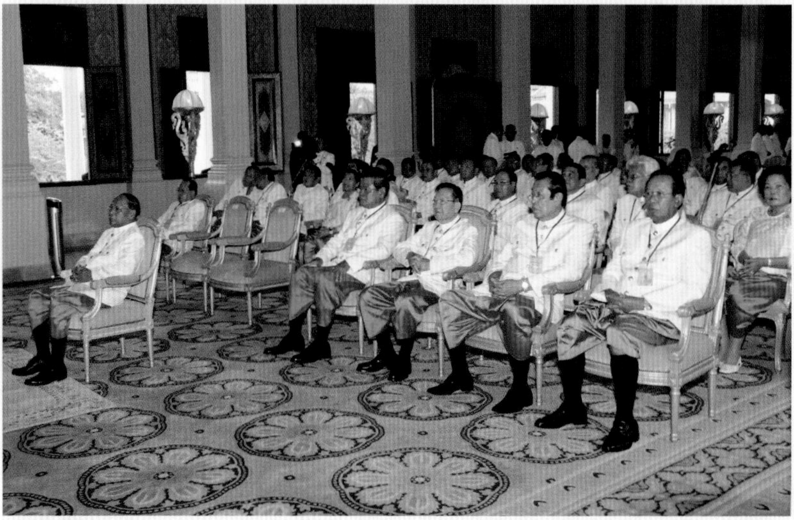

Attending the ceremony at the palace with other newly elected members of the National Assembly

Chairing a plenary session of the National Assembly with First Vice President Nguon Nhel (left) and Second Vice President Khuon Sudary (right) in 2013

Voting during a plenary session of the National Assembly. Prime Minister Samdech Hun Sen is in the front row, sixth from right. Other senior cabinet members (from right) are National Assembly-Senate Relations and Inspection Minister Men Sam An, Economy and Finance Minister Keat Chhon, National Defence Minister Tea Banh, Minister in Charge of the Office of the Council of Ministers Sok An and Interior Minister Sar Kheng (partly obscured).

Attending the Royal Ploughing Ceremony with His Majesty King Norodom Sihamoni and Senate President Samdech Say Chhum (left) at the Chea Sim University of Kamchay Mear in Prey Veng Province in 2017. Usually held in May, the ceremony marks the onset of the annual monsoon rains and the agricultural planting season.

(Left and right) Prey Veng Governor Chea Somethy arrives for the ceremony. The focus is on which items are consumed by two sacred oxen led to dishes containing corn, grass, mung beans, rice, alcohol, sesame seeds and water.

Meeting with Cote d'Ivoire President Alassane Ouattara (centre) and National Assembly President Guillaume Soro during an official visit to the West African country in 2014

Meeting with Thai Prime Minister Prayut Chan-o-cha in Bangkok in 2018

Bilateral meeting with Belarusian House of Representatives Chairman Vladimir Andreichenko in Minsk in 2012

Heading a Cambodian parliamentary delegation to a meeting with the National Assembly of Vietnam in Hanoi, 2017, with Deputy Prime Minister Men Sam An, head of the Cambodia-Vietnam Parliamentary Friendship Group (left), Women Parliamentarians Group Chairwoman Khuon Sudary (right) and Economy, Finance, Banking and Audit Commission Chairman Cheam Yeap (second from right)

Assuming the chairmanship of the Asia-Pacific Parliamentary Forum (APPF) from Vietnamese National Assembly Vice Chairwoman Nguyen Thi Kim Ngan in Phnom Penh in 2018 as Japanese Ambassador Hidehisa Horinouchi looks on. Founded at the initiative of former Japanese Prime Minister Yasuhiro Nakasone in 1993, APPF now has 27 member parliaments.

Heading the Cambodian delegation to the annual meeting of the ASEAN Inter-Parliamentary Assembly in Lombok, Indonesia, in 2012

Addressing the 127th Assembly of the Inter-Parliamentary Union (IPU) in Quebec City in 2012. Based in Geneva, the IPU dates back to 1889 and now has 178 member parliaments.

Signing agreement with Lao National Assembly President Pany Yathothou in Vientiane in 2016

Group photo from the 19th annual meeting of the Asia-Pacific Parliamentary Forum in Ulaanbaatar in 2011

Meeting with Chinese National People's Congress Chairman Wu Bangguo in Beijing in 2011

Addressing the annual meeting of the Inter-Parliamentary Union in Panama in 2011

Attending the second trilateral conference of Cambodian, Lao and Vietnamese front organisations in Vientiane in 2013 as president of the National Council of the Solidarity Front for the Development of the Cambodian Motherland. The meeting was chaired by Lao Vice President Bounnhang Vorachit (centre), who now serves as president as well as secretary general of the Lao People's Revolutionary Party, and also attended by Vietnam Fatherland Front Central Committee Chairman Nguyen Thien Nhan (left), now secretary of the Communist Party of Vietnam Committee in Ho Chi Minh City (left).

Meeting in Hanoi in 2014 with Nguyen Phu Trong, general secretary of the Central Committee of the Communist Party of Vietnam

Group photo from the 20th annual meeting of the Asia-Pacific Parliamentary Forum in Tokyo in 2012 with former Japanese prime minister Yasuhiro Nakasone (front row, centre), who founded the forum in 1993

Heading the Cambodian delegation to the 22nd annual meeting of the Asia-Pacific Parliamentary Forum in the Mexican City of Puerto Vallarta in 2014

Addressing the audience at the 28th anniversary of the foundation of the United Front, in Anlong Chrey on 2 December, 2006. The ceremony was organised by the Solidarity Front for the Development of the Cambodian Motherland, set up in 2006 to succeed the United Front for the Construction and Defence of the Kampuchean Homeland established in 1981.

Operating a bulldozer at the Anlong Chrey Redevelopment Village in 2009

Attending a house-blessing ceremony with monks for the new owners of a dwelling in Thlok Trach Redevelopment Village, one of 16 houses offered to the poor, on 6 and 7 April, 2013

My wife and I presenting the title for a new house to a villager in Thlok Trach Redevelopment Village. We offered 10 additional houses to the poor during ceremonies held on 26 and 28 May, 2014.

The new houses in Thlok Trach Redevelopment Village are located on new roads, and are based on traditional Khmer architectural designs for houses built from timber.

(Top and above) To mark my 80th birthday on 25 May, 2014, my wife and I received water blessings from Great Supreme Patriach Tep Vong who heads the Mahanikaya, the main Buddhist order in Cambodia.

(This page and opposite) To celebrate its 35th anniversary, we inaugurated a monument to the United Front for the National Salvation of Kampuchea that we founded on 2 December, 1978, to overthrow the genocidal Pol Pot régime. Located in Pi Thnou Commune in Snuol District in Kratie Province, the December 2 Memorial Monument was inaugurated by a People's Congress organised by the Solidarity Front for the Development of the Cambodian Motherland on 2 December, 2013.

With my wife Sao Ty

With members of my extended family

nual exports of Cambodian rice would reach one million tonnes by 2015. As for industry, we had 847 factories with 528,000 workers at the end of 2012, mainly in the garment, agro-industry, construction and electricity sectors. The number of foreigners visiting Cambodia had reached 3.5 million a year by 2012. Drawn by temples such as Angkor Wat and Preah Vihear in the post-war climate of social and political stability, the number of foreign visitors was soon forecast to reach 4 million.

The education sector had meanwhile grown exceptionally well. By 2012, we had 5,125 kindergartens, 6,849 primary schools, 1,196 junior high schools and 426 senior high schools. We also had 38 public and 59 private universities as well as another 20 public educational institutions and 32 private ones.

As for religion, Cambodia had 4,514 Buddhist temples with an estimated 56,820 monks in 2011. In addition, we had 392 mosques for the Muslim population – estimated at 320,419 – and 505 Christian churches with an estimated 93,688 followers. In the healthcare sector, we built infrastructure in provincial towns and eventually had health centres covering every commune. And in an achievement recognised by the World Health Organization (WHO), we reduced maternal and child mortality rates.

Since Liberation in 1979, I have personally contributed to the rehabilitation and rebuilding of the Cambodian motherland. In many cities and provinces, I have helped build Buddhist temples. I knew what it was like to be poor, having struggled in company with other villagers back in Anlong Chrey. Life was so difficult then. Deep in the forest, villagers were ignored by the authorities. They mostly subsisted on natural resources, leading unfulfilling lives. I was determined to reduce poverty.

I was also determined to repay the people and communities

who had sheltered my wife and me, as well as other people of all ages facing similar struggles. I had seen the complexity of territorial issues left behind by French colonial rule. In the spirit of solidarity, friendship and cooperation, I resolved to do my utmost – accompanied by Samdech Techo Hun Sen as head of government – to resolve border issues, ensuring that neighbouring countries shared benefits in accordance with neutral and fair changes in boundaries. With the agreement of the Joint Border Committee and the consent of the leaders of Cambodia and Vietnam, the border lines for 49 hectares in Anlong Chrey and 122 hectares in Thlok Trach have been settled. These two areas are now sovereign territory of the Kingdom of Cambodia. People are settled, earn their living and are no longer worried. Neither am I.

Aiming to improve people's livelihoods, I took initiatives to find ways of developing solid, well-marked and permanently stable borders, and so recognise the territory that had sheltered me from the enemy during the cause of national salvation.

I have dedicated myself to giving something back to the area where I grew up in Ponhea Kraek District, which had experienced so much sadness. So for Anlong Chrey, Thlok Trach and other villages, I have devoted myself to helping construct buildings along the border which represent our national cultural identity. These include dining halls and temples in the villages of Saam in Kraek Commune as well as Trapeang Phlong, Trapeang Pring and Kbal Damrey in Trapeang Phlong Commune where I also helped build a temple in the village of Trach Khaol. In Kak Commune, where I was born, I provided assistance to build schools and temples in the villages of Stueng Touch and Santey, along with a school and training school in the village of Ta Am. In Anlong Chrey and Thlok Trach villages, we inaugurated schools, administrative buildings, vocational training centres and homes for teachers on 2 December 2006, which marked the 28th anniversary of the founding of the Front. In March 2011 we opened a fully equipped health centre with a maternity ward. In several locations, irrigation systems have been built. The two villages, located along canals and surrounded by new roads, look particularly attractive.

American and South Vietnamese forces had been bombing Anlong Chrey since 1964. Since 2007, the village has been entirely rebuilt in a typical Khmer style, with houses on stilts in concrete and tiles, provided with toilets and wells. They officially came into use in May 2009.

The neighbouring village of Thlok Trach is about two kilometres south of Anlong Chrey. During the 1950s, 1960s and 1970s, it served as the revolutionary base for the Eastern Zone under the command of So Phim. Maps left by French colonial forces show the village entirely located inside Vietnamese territory. After the Paris Peace Agreements and democratic elections organised by UNTAC in 1993, the village of Thlok Trach became a flashpoint for the opposition to create conflict with Vietnam and the Cambodian People's Party. Vietnam responded by reinforcing its sovereignty. This affected the daily lives of local people, who faced increasing shortages as they could no longer gather vines in the forest or grow rice in distant fields. Some people became hostages to the opposition without being aware of the historical facts. After the border issue was resolved in May 2012, I commemorated the event by building canals, roads and numerous Khmer-style houses: these were inaugurated in June 2013. Hundreds of wooden houses were built for poor people in other villages.

Wat Thkov, formally known as Wat Kiri Sovannaram, has been rebuilt. Dating back to 1827, it was bombed and burnt to the ground by French colonial forces fighting Khmer Issarak revolutionaries in the 1950s. Like many other temples across the country, it was repaired after Liberation on 7 January 1979. The reconstruction work was, however, not robust, so it was renovated again between 2012 and 2014. The temple grounds include fences and gates, a dormitory and a dining hall as well as flags, shrines, courtyards, gardens, roads, lighting and a sewage system.

I also conserved the area around Tuol Preah Theat, building a shrine and statue of our ancestor Damkol Reach for people to worship according to traditional beliefs and customs. The seven hectares are fenced and surrounded by nature preserved as a heritage area. Public lighting and electricity connected to the national grid have been offered to the people at reasonable prices. To preserve the historic area and further improve local living standards, efforts have been made to promote private investment to transform these poor villages into agro-industrial areas with small and medium-sized enterprises and resorts.

With aid from friendly countries, our war-ravaged national road network has been rebuilt. We have also completed new roads, such as National Road No. 8 to the northeast provinces of Mondulkiri and Ratanakkiri as well as roads along the Cambodia-Thai border to the temples of Preah Vihear, Ta Moine and Ta Krobey. Many bridges have been built, notably the Koh Kong Bridge, the Sekong Bridge in Stung Treng and the Kizuna Bridge over the Mekong River in Kampong Cham. Others include the Prek Kdam Bridge and the New Chruoy Changva Bridge over the Tonle Sap River, the Prek Tameak Bridge over the Mekong and the New Monivong Bridge over the Bassac River. Travel is no longer difficult and time-consuming. With better connections between north and south and between east and west, people's standards of living have improved.

In addition, there have been hydropower plants built, such as those at Kamchay, Kirirom, Stung Russey Chrom, Stung Tatai and Atai and others are under construction. These contribute to national development.

Urban development in the capital and cities around the country has moved forward, with the appearance of modern apartments, condominiums, houses and shopping malls as well as dozens of high-rise buildings. Visiting world leaders welcome the country's rapid development.

Most Cambodians acknowledge that progress and international prestige would never have been achieved without the United Front for the National Salvation of Kampuchea (now known as the Solidarity Front for the Development of the Cambodian Motherland) established on 2 December 1978, as well as the Cambodian People's Party led by Samdech Chea Sim, Samdech Hun Sen and myself, and the Liberation of 7 January 1979.

My efforts were dedicated to the homeland and the people who had suffered endlessly from repression – the shelling and bombing during the French colonial period in the 1950s, and by South Vietnamese and American forces in 1964 that killed and separated so many people. That wretched ordeal lasted until late 1978, by which time Pol Pot's régime had burnt everything to the ground.

The final phase of suffering was immeasurably horrific. Regardless of whether they were adults or children, male or female, old or young, so many people were tortured to death, day and night. The massive forced evacuations made people so desperate they were just waiting to die.

Cambodian people are always reminded to be grateful for what they have, and to pass this sense of gratitude on to the next generation. I'm convinced that people will always remember the

Khmer saying: 'When drinking water, don't forget the source and when eating fruit, don't forget those who plant the trees.' After the enormous suffering during decades of war, tragedy and internal conflict, I have one desire only: that future leaders never repeat the mistakes of the past. We must do our utmost to ensure security, stability, peace, progress and development – and protect our sovereignty and territorial integrity for ever.

DECORATIONS AWARDED TO THE AUTHOR

National

Medal of National Merit
Medal of Independence
Grand Cross of the Royal Order of the Kingdom of Cambodia
Grand Cross of the Royal Order of Sowathara
Grand Cross of the Royal Order of Her Majesty Preah Kossomak Nearyrath
Sena Jayaseddh Medals
National Defence Medals (three gold, three silver and three bronze)

International

Joliot-Curie Gold Peace Medal of the World Peace Council
Medals from Bulgaria, Cuba, Lao People's Democratic Republic, Mongolia, Nicaragua, Palestine, Philippines, Poland and the Soviet Union

APPENDIX 1

The Cambodian constitution that came into effect in September 1993 was adopted by a Constituent Assembly formed after national elections four months earlier. Between 1993 and 2013, the Cambodian National Assembly served five parliamentary terms.

National Assembly of the Kingdom of Cambodia (1993–2013)

I. Constituent Assembly

After the signing of the Paris Peace Agreements on 23 October 1991, all four Cambodian factions reached a consensus to nominate His Royal Highness Prince Norodom Sihanouk, considered the father of national reconciliation, as president of a Supreme National Council (SNC). This was in accordance with the agreement to establish a United Nations Transitional Authority in Cambodia (UNTAC) to perform civilian and military duties while respecting the country's territorial sovereignty and integrity.

Between 23 and 28 May 1993, 90 per cent of eligible Cambodians took part in free and fair elections organised with the support of UNTAC. Held in an impartial political atmosphere with full respect for Cambodia's sovereignty, the elections were based on proportional representation with 39 parties contesting 120 seats in 21 provinces and municipalities. The results were:

1. Funcinpec: 58 seats
2. Cambodian People's Party: 51 seats
3. Buddhist Liberal Democratic Party: 10 seats
4. Moulinaka: 1 seat

After the results were announced and recognised, a Constituent Assembly was formed on 13 June under the leadership of His Royal Highness Prince Sihanouk, the SNC president, with the participation of UNTAC Chief of Mission Yasushi Akashi, the Special Representative of the UN Secretary-General in Cambodia.

Samdech Son Sann (Buddhist Liberal Democratic Party) became president of the Constituent Assembly with His Excellency Chea Sim (Cambodian People's Party) serving as first vice president and His Excellency Ing Kiet (Funcinpec) as second vice president. The assembly developed internal rules and a standing committee was formed to draft a new constitution consistent with the history and spirit of the Khmer nation.

After a six-day debate, the Constituent Assembly adopted a draft constitution on 21 September with a majority vote of more than two-thirds. The constitution was promulgated and came into effect on 24 September with His Majesty King Norodom Sihanouk as monarch in full respect of the Cambodian people's rights and true democracy.

II. First Legislature (1993–1998)

When the constitution came into effect, the Constituent Assembly became the National Assembly. The allocation of seats in the First Legislature of the National Assembly under the new constitution (Article 55) was identical to that of the Constituent Assembly and included seven women. His Excellency Chea Sim (Cambodian People's Party) was elected president, His Excellency Loy Sim Chheang (Funcinpec) first vice president, and His Excellency Son Soubert (Buddhist Liberal Democratic Party) second vice president.

The National Assembly has legislative powers and performs its roles and duties in accordance with the constitution and existing laws. After 1993, it was responsible for:

- adopting the constitution, lifting parliamentary immunity or extending the legislative term by one year with a two-thirds majority of all members;
- adopting votes of confidence in the government or dissolving the government by majority of vote of all members; and
- questioning the government (the National Assembly allocates one day a week for questions and debate).

The first legislature had a 12-member permanent committee comprising the president, the two vice presidents and the chairmen of nine parliamentary commissions.

The first legislature adopted 90 laws.

III. Second Legislature (1998–2003)

The second legislature under the new constitution followed elections on 26 July 1998 under a proportional system based on 23 provinces and municipalities (including the new municipalities of Kep and Pailin), with the participation of 39 parties. The results were:

1. Cambodian People's Party: 64 seats
2. Funcinpec: 43 seats
3. Sam Rainsy Party: 15 seats

The new National Assembly had 122 members including 15 women. The second legislature convened its first session in Siem Reap on 22 September under His Majesty King Sihanouk to declare the validity of the legitimate mandate and to take official oaths.

His Royal Highness Prince Norodom Ranariddh (Funcinpec) was elected president, Samdech Heng Samrin (Cambodian People's Party) first vice president, and His Excellency Chem Snguon (Cambodian People's Party) second vice president.

The 12-member permanent committee again comprised the president, two vice presidents and chairmen of the nine commissions.

The second legislature adopted 88 laws.

IV. Third Legislature (2003–2008)

The third legislature followed elections on 23 July 2003 under a proportional system based on 24 provinces and municipalities (including the new province of Oddar Meanchey). Three of the 23 participating parties won seats:

1. Cambodian People's Party: 73 seats
2. Funcinpec: 26 seats
3. Sam Rainsy Party: 24 seats

The new National Assembly had 123 members including 24 women. The third legislature held its first session on 27 September under Samdech Chea Sim, the acting head of state, with the participation of 73 members from the Cambodian People's Party. Members from Funcinpec and the Sam Rainsy Party boycotted the session.

As the oldest member, His Excellency Chea Soth presided over the declaration of validity of the legitimate mandate on 15 December with the participation of 118 members. On the same day, 122 members took their official oaths.

The Cambodian People's Party was initially unable to command a two-thirds majority to form a government as Funcinpec, its coalition partner in the previous legislature, signed an alliance agreement with the opposition Sam Rainsy Party. A deadlock ensued for more than a year until Funcinpec abandoned its agreement with the opposition party and entered into negotiations with the ruling party.

The first parliamentary session of the third legislature was presided over by His Excellency Chea Soth on 8 July 2004 with 96 of the 123 members taking part. The session adopted additional provisions to the constitution to ensure the normal functioning of national organisations. These comprised six articles stating procedures for package votes and were proclaimed by Royal Kram No. NS/RKM/0704/001 dated 13 July.

On 15 July, a package vote held under His Excellency Chea Soth elected the president and vice presidents of the assembly as well as the chairmen of the commissions. A vote of confidence in the Royal Government won the approval of 96 out of 96 votes.

His Royal Highness Prince Norodom Ranariddh was elected president, Samdech Heng Samrin first vice president, and His Excellency Nguon Nhel (Cambodian People's Party) second vice president.

As mutual trust between the Cambodian People's Party and Funcinpec deteriorated, a war of words broke out. To resolve the political deadlocks that had affected the second and third legislatures and to show the determination of the Cambodian People's Party to maintain peace and political stability, Samdech Hun Sen, the prime minister, and Samdech Heng Samrin initiated a proposal to amend several provisions of the constitution to replace the two-thirds majority rule with a requirement for an absolute majority (50 per cent + 1 vote). The initiative was supported by Funcinpec and the Sam Rainsy Party, which hoped to topple the Cambodian People's Party in the next election. The amendments involved Article 82 of the constitution, six new articles – Articles 88, 90, 98, 106, 111 and 114, and Article 6 of the additional provisions to the constitution related to erasing the requirement for a two-thirds majority and replacing it with an absolute majority (50 per cent + 1 vote) and changing parliamentary quorums from more than two-thirds to more than a half of all members.

The National Assembly adopted the amendments on 2 March 2006 in the fourth plenary session of the third legislature with the approval of 96 of the 97 attending members and proclaimed by Royal Kram No. NS/RKM/0306/006 dated 9 March 2006.

A day after the adoption of the amendments, His Royal Highness Prince Ranariddh (Funcinpec) resigned as president of the National Assembly which, in turn, elected Samdech Heng Samrin as his successor on 21 March with the approval of 112 votes of all members attending. The assembly elected His Excellency Nguon Nhel first vice president and His Excellency Hong Sun Huot (Funcinpec) second vice president (to replace His Excellency You Hokry at the end of the legislature).

V. Fourth Legislature (2008–2013)

The fourth legislature under the new constitution followed national elections on 27 July 2008 under a proportional system based on the same 24 provinces and municipalities as the previous election. Five of the 11 participating parties won seats:

1. Cambodian People's Party: 90 seats
2. Sam Rainsy Party: 26 seats
3. Human Rights Party: 3 seats
4. Funcinpec: 2 seats
5. Norodom Ranariddh Party: 2 seats

The new National Assembly had 123 members, including 26 women. The fourth legislature opened its first session presided over by His Majesty King Norodom Sihamoni at the new National Assembly building on 24 September 2008 with the participation of 119 members to declare the validity of the legitimate mandate and take official oaths.

Samdech Akak Moha Ponhea Chakrei Heng Samrin was re-elected president, His Excellency Nguon Nhel first vice president, and His Excellency Say Chhum (Cambodian People's Party) second vice president (succeeded by Her Excellency Khuon Sudary in April 2012).

The fourth legislature adopted 83 laws, and had the following nine parliamentary commissions.

1. Commission on Human Rights, Reception of Complaints, Investigation and National Assembly–Senate Relations
2. Commission on Economy, Finance, Banking and Audit
3. Commission on Planning, Investment, Agriculture, Rural Development, Environment and Water Resources
4. Commission on Interior, National Defence, Investigation and Public Functions
5. Commission on Foreign Affairs, International Cooperation, Information and Media
6. Commission on Legislation and Justice
7. Commission on Education, Youth and Sports, Cults and Religious Affairs, Culture and Tourism
8. Commission on Health, Social Affairs and Veterans, Youth Rehabilitation, Labour, Vocational Training and Women's Affairs
9. Commission on Public Works and Transport, Telecommunications and Posts, Industry, Mining and Energy, Commerce, Land Management, Urban Planning and Construction

APPENDIX 2

Overseas activities and key international forums involving Samdech Chakrei Heng Samrin as President of the National Assembly of the Kingdom of Cambodia

I. ASEAN Inter-Parliamentary Assembly (AIPA)

As president of the National Assembly, Samdech Chakrei Heng Samrin led delegations to seven general assemblies of AIPA and its predecessor, the ASEAN Inter-Parliamentary Organisation (AIPO), between 2006 and 2012, including the 32nd in Phnom Penh, which he chaired in 2011:

27th General Assembly of AIPO in Cebu (Philippines), 10–15 September 2006;
28th General Assembly of AIPA in Kuala Lumpur (Malaysia), 19–24 August 2007;
29th General Assembly of AIPA in Singapore, 19–24 August 2008;
30th General Assembly of AIPA in Pattaya (Thailand), 2–8 August 2009;
31st General Assembly of AIPA in Hanoi (Vietnam), 20–24 September 2010;
32nd General Assembly of AIPA in Phnom Penh (Cambodia), 18–24 September 2011; and
33rd General Assembly of AIPA in Lombok (Indonesia), 16–22 September 2012.

Samdech Chakrei Heng Samrin also led Cambodian delegations to two other AIPA meetings: the Extraordinary Meeting of the AIPA Executive Committee in Kuala Lumpur, Malaysia, 16–19 April 2007, and the Meeting between ASEAN Heads of State/Government and the AIPA Delegation during the 18th ASEAN Summit in Jakarta, Indonesia, 5–8 May 2011.

II. Inter-Parliamentary Union (IPU)

Samdech Chakrei Heng Samrin led Cambodian delegations to the following IPU assemblies between 2006 and 2012:

114th Assembly, Nairobi (Kenya), 7–12 May 2006, under the theme *Promoting Democracy and Helping to Build Democratic Institutions*;
116th Assembly, Bali (Indonesia), 29 April–4 May 2007, under the theme *Global Warming: Ten Years after Kyoto*;
118th Assembly, Cape Town (South Africa), 13–18 April 2008, under the theme *Pushing Back the Frontiers of Poverty*;

120th Assembly, Addis Ababa (Ethiopia), 5–10 April 2009, under the theme *Parliaments: Building Peace, Democracy and Development in Times of Crisis*;
121st Assembly, Geneva (Switzerland), 19–21 October 2009
124th Assembly, Panama City (Panama), 15–20 April 2011, under the theme *Parliamentary Accountability: Living Up to People's Expectations*; and
127th Assembly, Quebec City (Canada), 21–26 October 2012, under the theme *Citizenship, Identity and Linguistic and Cultural Diversity in a Globalised World.*

III. Asia Pacific Parliamentary Forum (APPF)

In addition, Samdech Chakrei Heng Samrin led Cambodian delegations to the following APPF annual meetings between 2007 and 2012:

15th Annual Meeting of AAPF in Moscow (Russian Federation) with the participation of 117 members of parliamen (MPs) from 24 countries, 20–24 January 2007;
16th Annual Meeting of APPF in Auckland (New Zealand), with the participation of 146 MPs from 28 countries, 20–25 January 2008;
17th Annual Meeting of APPF in Vientiane (Lao People's Democratic Republic) with the participation of 128 MPs from 22 countries, 11–15 January 2009;
18th Annual Meeting of APPF in Singapore, with the participation of 121 MPs from 21 countries, 17–21 January 2010;
19th Annual Meeting of APPF in Ulaanbaatar (Mongolia), with the participation of 107 MPs from 19 countries; 23–27 January 2011; and
20th Annual Meeting of APPF in Tokyo (Japan), with participants from 19 countries, 8–12 January 2012.

INDEX